Data Integration Life Cycle Management with SSIS

A Short Introduction by Example

Andy Leonard

Apress®

Data Integration Life Cycle Management with SSIS

Andy Leonard
Farmville, Virginia, USA

ISBN-13 (pbk): 978-1-4842-3275-0   ISBN-13 (electronic): 978-1-4842-3276-7
https://doi.org/10.1007/978-1-4842-3276-7

Library of Congress Control Number: 2017960764

Cover image designed by Freepik

Managing Director: Welmoed Spahr
Editorial Director: Todd Green
Acquisitions Editor: Jonathan Gennick
Development Editor: Laura Berendson
Coordinating Editor: Jill Balzano
Copy Editor: Mary Behr
Compositor: SPi Global
Indexer: SPi Global
Artist: SPi Global

Distributed to the book trade worldwide by Springer Science+Business Media New York, 233 Spring Street, 6th Floor, New York, NY 10013. Phone 1-800-SPRINGER, fax (201) 348-4505, e-mail orders-ny@springer-sbm.com, or visit www.springeronline.com. Apress Media, LLC is a California LLC and the sole member (owner) is Springer Science + Business Media Finance Inc (SSBM Finance Inc). SSBM Finance Inc is a **Delaware** corporation.

For information on translations, please e-mail rights@apress.com, or visit www.apress.com/rights-permissions.

Apress titles may be purchased in bulk for academic, corporate, or promotional use. eBook versions and licenses are also available for most titles. For more information, reference our Print and eBook Bulk Sales web page at www.apress.com/bulk-sales.

Any source code or other supplementary material referenced by the author in this book is available to readers on GitHub via the book's product page, located at www.apress.com/9781484232750. For more detailed information, please visit www.apress.com/source-code.

Printed on acid-free paper

For Christy.

The original version of this book was revised. An erratum to this book can be found at
https://doi.org/10.1007/978-1-4842-3276-7_13

Table of Contents

About the Author

Andy Leonard is Chief Data Engineer at Enterprise Data & Analytics. He also is an SSIS trainer, consultant, and developer. Andy is a Business Intelligence Markup Language (Biml) developer and BimlHero. He is also a SQL Server database and data warehouse developer, community mentor, engineer, and farmer. Andy is a co-author of *SQL Server Integration Services Design Patterns* and *The Biml Book*.

Acknowledgments

I thank God first for He leads me in right paths for his name's sake (Psalm 23:3). I thank Christy, my lovely bride, and our children—Stevie Ray, Emma, and Riley—for sacrificing some Dad time. Thanks to the awesome team at Enterprise Data & Analytics for their patience and hard work while I wrote: Kent Bradshaw, Nick Harris, and Penny Trupe. I also have an awesome team at Apress: Jill Balzano kept the wheels on the bus going 'round and 'round and Jonathan Gennick is the best editor in the business.

Foreword

I've had the honor and privilege of knowing and working with Andy Leonard for several years. Most of that time has been spent collaborating on projects as independent contractors. We've watched and learned as SSIS has matured through the years. Andy is one of the most knowledgeable and technically savvy people that I've had the pleasure of working with. And, with close to 40 years in the field, I've worked with a lot of people.

This book is filled with best practices we learned through years of trial and error with the practical application of SSIS to solve real problems. We learned by doing and then rethinking to look for better solutions. Things change quickly so we learn new things all the time. We are constantly reevaluating what we've done in the past and comparing it with what we've learned since then.

Data Integration Life Cycle Management with SSIS grew out of the many iterations working on various projects. It's not just about development but also the effort of ongoing maintenance. Understanding both sides is critical in developing processes that work well in the DevOps enterprise. This approach is a methodology that helps make the development and deployment processes more efficient, effective, and predictable. That makes us all a little happier.

This book is also about sharing what has been learned along the journey with others who can benefit from it. Andy is all about that, and it's one of the things that I appreciate most about him. I sincerely hope that you find this book helpful now and for a long to come.

Enjoy!

Kent Bradshaw
Providence Forge, VA
Summer 2017

CHAPTER 1

Introduction to DILM

DevOps is a combination of the words "Development" and "Operations." DevOps is about process improvement, which manifests in faster time to market, higher quality, repeatable automation, and code that is easier to support and maintain. Software testing is a major part of DevOps, starting with unit-testing conducted by software developers. Software testing occurs at all enterprise application tiers (Development, Quality Assurance, User Acceptance, Production, etc.). DevOps developers support Operations by surfacing process instrumentation and building repeatable configurations scripts. Configurations scripting supports higher quality and faster disaster recovery, and rapidly and reliably adding enterprise application tiers.

Software developers follow best practices to build robust enterprise software. For decades, developers have applied a collection of best practices called application lifecycle management, or *ALM*, when building applications. What is ALM? Application lifecycle management includes design principles that support DevOps. An important development concept is *separation of concerns*, design best practices including externalization (parameterization) and decoupling.

Data integration is moving data from one location to another. Data is often collected from disparate sources and loaded into a database to support centralized reporting. The reporting databases are known by different names in different enterprises: operational data store (ODS),

The original version of this chapter was revised. An erratum to this chapter can be found at https://doi.org/10.1007/978-1-4842-3276-7_13

© Andy Leonard 2018
A. Leonard, *Data Integration Life Cycle Management with SSIS*,
https://doi.org/10.1007/978-1-4842-3276-7_1

staging database, central repository, data warehouse (DW), or enterprise data warehouse (EDW), to list a few.

Data integration *is* software development. Data integration lifecycle management, or *DILM*, is the art and science of managing data integration in the modern DevOps enterprise. In this book, I share what I've learned managing SQL Server Integration Services (SSIS) data integration solutions in enterprises large and small.

My goal in writing this book is to teach you how to manage SSIS in your enterprise. As with all other software development platforms, lifecycle management is a best practice with SSIS. As with all other software development, it's possible to practice DevOps with SSIS.

Some History

SQL Server Integration Services (SSIS) was released in November 2005. Development on SSIS started long before, and I'm told the product was originally slated to be dubbed Data Transformation Services (DTS) 2.0. Many assemblies sport the namespace "Dts."

I want to introduce this book by making a few statements about SSIS.

SSIS Is a Software Development Platform

I cannot recall how many times I've seen job postings for database administrators "with SSIS experience."

Database administrator, database developer, and SSIS developer are different roles.

I cringe a little when I read said postings. SSIS is a software development platform and I am a software developer. I am also a database developer. I am *not* a database administrator (DBA). I've tried to do the job of a DBA and failed. Miserably. It's not that I don't appreciate the role of a DBA; I promise I do. Some of my best friends are DBAs. I want to begin by expressing to you this simple truth: DBA, database developer, and SSIS developer are different roles.

SSIS Is an Enterprise Data Integration Engine

SSIS is designed to move data from one location to another, which is the essence of data integration. Data integration can include reshaping, cleansing, and transformation of data; but at its heart, data integration is data relocation. The SSIS Data Flow Task was revolutionary when it was introduced. In my humble opinion, it remains pretty slick technology. The pipeline architecture surfaces most of the levers one needs to tweak to achieve enterprise scale.

Is SSIS the perfect data integration engine for *every* data integration need? No. But it is an amazingly flexible solution to most data integration requirements.

A number of times I've accomplished what-cannot-be-done with SSIS. Years ago I even got into a flame war online with a really smart, internet-famous software developer who wrote a post listing all the things wrong with SSIS. I shared with this individual that I teach people SSIS and all my students know the solution to almost every item listed in the post.

> *Someone recently asked me, "When is Microsoft going to deliver an enterprise data integration engine?" My response? "2005."*
>
> – Andy Leonard

SSIS Is Difficult to Learn

How do I know? I (and others) have made a living for more than a decade teaching people how to use SSIS.

All software platforms have "corners," - quirks and edge cases that the language just isn't the best at managing. SSIS has about 30 corners. I describe the data flow task to students in this manner: "SSIS wants you to *think* like a data flow and thinking like a data flow is hard."

"SSIS wants you to think like a data flow."

Lifecycle Management

SSIS, even at the time of this writing, is difficult to manage in the enterprise lifecycle. Exhibit A is comparing SSIS packages. SSIS is XML-based. XML is a self-describing data format with less respect for order than traditional data stores. For example, the following XML snippets are equivalent:

```
<Book>
    <Title>Data Integration Lifecycle Management</Title>
    <Author>Andy Leonard</Author>
    <Year>2017</Year>
</Book>
<Book>
    <Author>Andy Leonard</Author>
    <Title>Data Integration Lifecycle Management</Title>
    <Year>2017</Year>
</Book>
```

You may look at this example and quip, "But Andy, I can figure out that these data are equivalent just by looking at them." You are correct; examining five rows of data is pretty simple. Imagine looking at five hundred rows of XML, with tags and attributes in a different order, and you begin to understand the complexity of comparing XML data.

XML is not bad or wrong. XML's semi-structured nature makes SSIS difficult to compare.

Solutions and Credit Where Credit Is Due

The remainder of this book focuses on solutions. With the exception of the BimlExpress Metadata Framework, Kent Bradshaw, Kevin Hazzard, and I developed the solutions contained in this book. Scott Currie and his team at Varigence, Inc. built Business Intelligence Markup Language (Biml) and taught us how to author Biml. Some of what Scott and his team taught us made its way into the BimlExpress Metadata Framework.

A more accurate rendering of the facts is that Kent, Kevin, and I learned what we know from experience and from others. In a very real sense, none of us is *self-taught*. Rather, we are *community-taught*.

Some of these solutions are simply ways of using the technology Microsoft shipped "in the box" with SSIS. Some are best practices. Some are manual and others are automated. Some are free tools and utilities by vendors. Some are free utilities and tools the team at Enterprise Data & Analytics (`entdna.com`), Tudor Data Solutions (`tudords.com`), and DevJourney (`devjourney.com`) have developed; many are part of the DILM Suite (`dilmsuite.com`). One, BimlExpress, is a third-party product from Varigence (`varigence.com`). A couple, SSIS Framework Community Edition and BimlExpress Metadata Framework, are free versions of for-sale implemented solutions that Enterprise Data & Analytics sells as part of consulting engagements.

Do we have all the answers? Goodness no! We have some. Like you, we learn new stuff every day. Here in this book is some of what we know today.

CHAPTER 2

SSIS

This book is not intended to teach you SSIS. If you read this book and work through the examples, you may learn more about SSIS. That is my hope, but it's not my goal in writing this book to teach you SSIS. My goal is teach you how to *manage* SSIS in your enterprise. If you desire to learn SSIS, I recommend the *Stairway to Integration Services at SQL Server Central* (sqlservercentral.com/stairway/72494/) for beginners and *SQL Server Integration Services Design Patterns* (amazon.com/Server-Integration-Services-Design-Patterns/dp/1484200837) for more advanced learning.

Learning by example is best. In this chapter, you will build an SSIS project for demonstration purposes. This SSIS project will include one SSIS package, a connection manager, variables, project parameters, and package parameters. You will use this SSIS project, DILMSample, throughout the remainder of this book. The SSIS project is built in SQL Server Data Tools (SSDT). Please see Appendix A for links to the tools and utilities you will use throughout this book.

I will discuss data integration instrumentation and messaging to surface log messages during the execution of the SSIS package. These messages serve people troubleshooting failed executions and surface important data integration instrumentation metadata.

© Andy Leonard 2018
A. Leonard, *Data Integration Life Cycle Management with SSIS*,
https://doi.org/10.1007/978-1-4842-3276-7_2

The Demo

Open SSDT and create a new SSIS project named DILMSample. When SSDT creates a new SSIS project, it loads a default SSIS project. The default SSIS project includes

- Project parameters, stored in the Project.params file

- A virtual folder for project-scope connection managers

- A virtual folder for package parts

  - A virtual folder for control flow package parts

- A virtual folder for miscellaneous items

- A default (empty) SSIS package named Package.dtsx

Rename Package.dtsx as SimplePackage.dtsx, as shown in Figure 2-1.

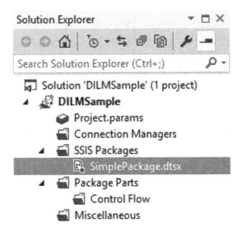

Figure 2-1. *The DILMSample SSIS project*

Renaming the package communicates intent; leaving the default package name communicates laziness.

Adding Package Parameters

Since we plan to use this project and package to demonstrate lifecycle management, let's add parameters. To start, click the Parameters tab on the SimplePackage.dtsx package. Add two package parameters with the settings shown in Table 2-1.

Table 2-1. *Package Parameter Settings*

Name	Data type	Value	Sensitive	Required	Description
IntPkgParam	Int32	42	False	False	
StringPkgParam	String	Hi There!	False	False	

When completed, your Parameters tab should appear similar to that shown in Figure 2-2.

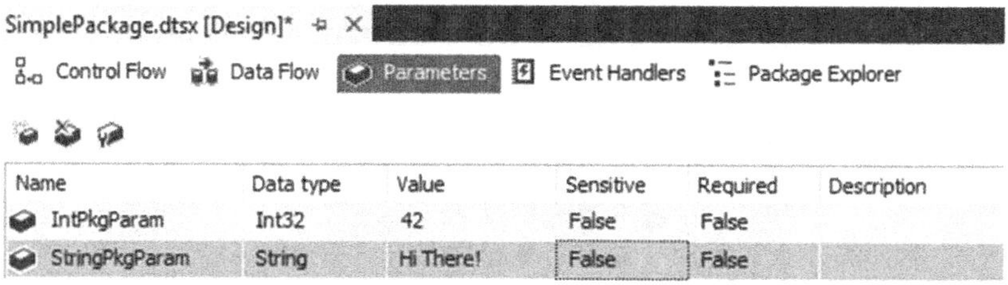

Figure 2-2. *Package parameters*

You add these demo parameters at the package scope. *Scope* is an important concept in software development *and* lifecycle management. The "Dev" part of DevOps focuses on building code that is easily manageable by Operations. How does scope help? Later you will *externalize* parameter values into Transact-SQL (T-SQL) scripts. Operations personnel will ultimately manage externalized values by deploying and maintaining T-SQL scripts. One goal of DevOps development is to communicate as much information as possible to

9

Operations people, especially Operations people who have no idea how
SSIS works. Scoping parameters and variables to their proper level (no
higher or lower) communicates where and how parameter values are used
in the SSIS application, thus shedding some light on the "black box" of the
data integration project.

Adding Project Parameters

Open the Project Parameters window by double-clicking the Project.
params artifact in Solution Explorer, shown in Figure 2-3.

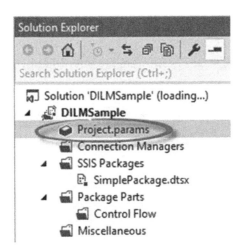

Figure 2-3. *Project parameters*

Add two project parameters with the settings from Table 2-2.

Table 2-2. *Project Parameter Settings*

Name	Data type	Value	Sensitive	Required	Description
IntProjParam	Int32	-99	False	False	
StringProjParam	String	A project parameter	False	False	

When completed your Project Parameters tab should appear similar to that shown in Figure 2-4.

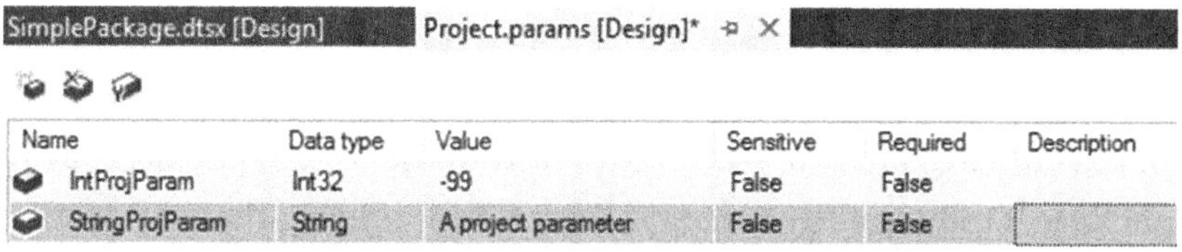

Figure 2-4. *Project parameters*

SSIS parameters work a lot like SSIS variables. There are two important distinctions:

1. SSIS variable values may be changed at any time, before or during SSIS package execution. SSIS parameter values may be changed before SSIS package execution but not during SSIS package execution.

2. SSIS parameter values may be marked as *sensitive* or *required*. Sensitive parameters are encrypted. Required parameters must be overridden before SSIS package execution.

11

A Note About Variables, Parameters, and Scope

Create SSIS variables for values that will change during SSIS package execution, such as variables used in Foreach Loop container assignments.

Create package-scope parameters for values used in a single SSIS package. Package-scope parameter values cannot change during SSIS package execution. Create project-scope parameters for values that are shared across all (or several) SSIS packages in the SSIS project.

Save and close the Project Parameters window.

Adding an Execute SQL Task

Add an Execute SQL Task to the control flow of the SimplePackage.dtsx SSIS package. Open the Execute SQL Task Editor and set the ConnectionType property to ADO.NET. Click the Connection property and then click <New connection...>. The ADO.Net Connection Manager Editor opens. You can configure the ADO.Net connection manager to connect to any SQL Server database you desire. You are going to execute a generic query that will work with any SQL Server relational database.

I am using a virtual machine named vmDemo. I have an instance of SQL Server 2016 installed named vmDemo\Demo. I configured my ADO.Net connection manager to connect to a database named TestDB, as shown in Figure 2-5.

Figure 2-5. *Configuring an ADO.Net connection manager*

Click OK until you return to the Execute SQL Task Editor. Click in the Value textbox of the SQLStatement property and then click the ellipsis to open the Enter SQL Query dialog. In this dialog enter the following Transact-SQL statement:

```
Select Count(*) As TableCount
From [sys].[tables]
```

Why alias the value of Count(*)? The Execute SQL task expects return values in a tabular format with column names, especially if assigned to an SSIS variable (which is next).

13

Change the ResultSet property from None to Single Row. Click the Result Set page in the listbox on the left side of the Execute SQL Task Editor. Click the Add button and change the Result Name from NewResultName to 0. Click the dropdown in the Variable Name column beside the 0 Result Name and click <New variable...> to open the Add Variable dialog. Make sure the Container is set to SimplePackage. Name the variable TableCount and set the Value type property to Int32. Supply a default Value of 0. Your Add Variable dialog should appear as shown in Figure 2-6.

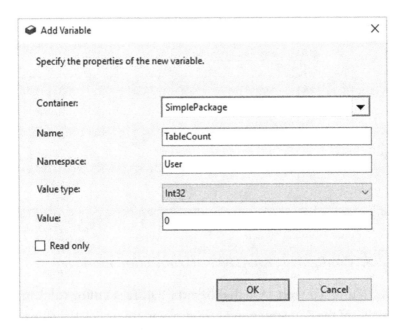

Figure 2-6. Adding a new SSIS variable

You may select the scope of the SSIS variable using the Container dropdown in the Add Variable dialog. Pay attention to this setting. If the Execute SQL task resides in a Sequence container, it is easy to accidentally scope a variable to the host Sequence container instead of the SSIS package.

A Note About SSIS Variable Scope

Because SSIS variables are rarely scoped beneath the SSIS package, the Microsoft SSIS Development Team changed the default behavior for SSIS variable scope. Before the change, SSIS variable scope defaulted to the executable with focus. SSIS variable scope now defaults to the SSIS package, *except in Add Variable dialogs*.

Click the OK button. Your Execute SQL Task Editor's Result Set page should appear as shown in Figure 2-7.

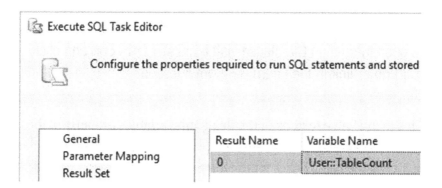

Figure 2-7. *A Result Set, configured*

Click the OK button to close the Execute SQL Task Editor. Right-click the Execute SQL task and click Rename. Rename the task "SQL Get Table Count".

Adding a Script Task

Add a Script task to SimplePackage.dtsx's Control Flow. Rename it "SCR Log Values" and connect an OnSuccess precedence constraint from the SQL Get Table Count Execute SQL task to the SCR Log Values Script task. Open the Script Task Editor. You can select Microsoft Visual Basic as the ScriptLanguage property or accept the default of Microsoft Visual C#. The demos in this book will use C#.

Why C#?

Since late 2016 Microsoft has repeatedly communicated that Visual Basic and C# language functionality will *diverge* (blogs.msdn.microsoft.com/dotnet/2017/02/01/the-net-language-strategy/). Microsoft's stated opinion (from the link) is that it will continue to evolve C# as a "state of the art programming language" while other features won't be added to Visual Basic because "they wouldn't address a need or fit naturally in VB." Please read the post and the links contained therein. C# and VB will be different moving forward, and C# will get features that will not be available in VB.

For a good tutorial on C#, please visit bimlscript.com and click the C# Primer link in the Learn Biml Now! lesson.

Click in the Value textbox of the ReadOnlyVariables property of the Script Task Editor, and then click the ellipsis to open the Select Variables dialog. Check the checkboxes for the following variables:

- System::TaskName
- System::PackageName
- User::TableCount
- $Package::IntPkgParam
- $Package::StringPkgParam
- $Project::IntProjParam
- $Project::StringProjParam

When completed, your Select Variables dialog should appear similar to that shown in Figure 2-8.

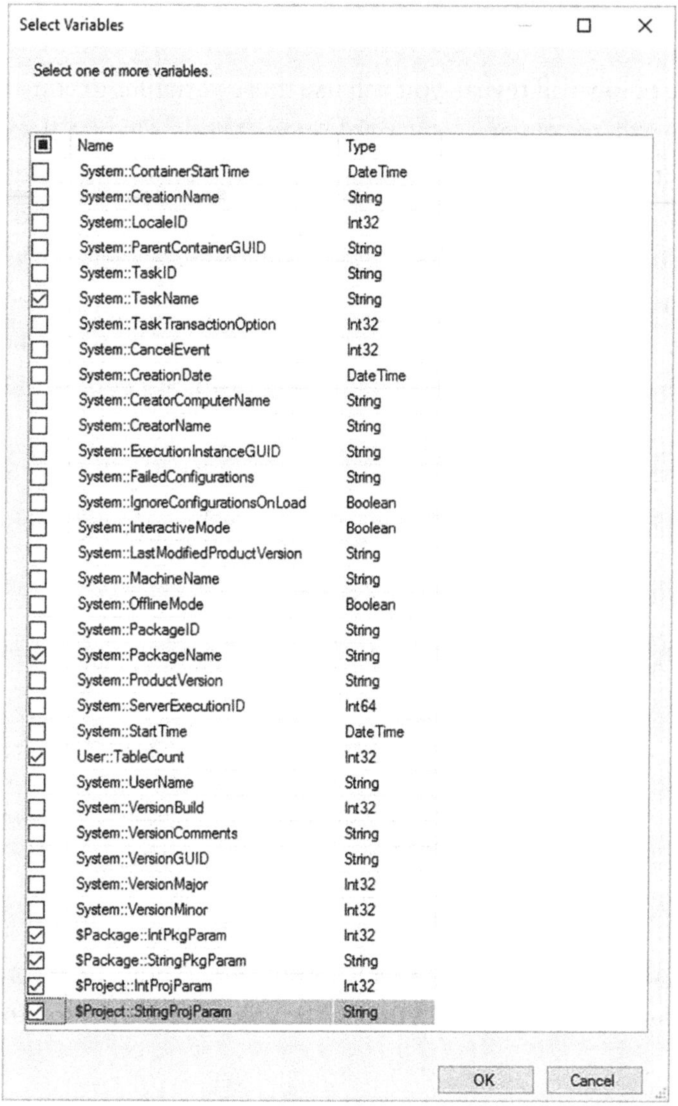

Figure 2-8. *The Select Variables dialog*

Why ProjectName and TaskName?

As the code below will reveal, you will use these variables to construct a value in the subComponent .Net variable in your code. Do you absolutely *need* this variable for SSIS development? No. But you absolutely need this variable if you are going to help the Operations team monitor and report messages and failures from SSIS logs. For the developer side of DevOps, it's a few lines of code. For the Operations side of DevOps, it surfaces one more piece of execution metadata in the logs. Providing this kind and level of process instrumentation is vital to the successful integration of DevOps and SSIS.

Click the OK button to close the Select Variables dialog. Your Script Task Editor should now appear as shown in Figure 2-9.

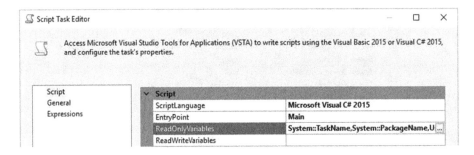

Figure 2-9. *The Script Task Editor*

Click the Edit Script button to open the Visual Studio Tools for Applications (VSTA) Editor. Edit the public void Main() method to read as follows:

```
public void Main()
{
        string packageName = Dts.Variables["System::Package
        Name"].Value.ToString();
        string taskName = Dts.Variables["System::Task
        Name"].Value.ToString();
```

```
string subComponent = packageName + "." + taskName;
bool fireAgain = true;

int tableCount = Convert.ToInt32(Dts.Variables
["User::TableCount"].Value);
int intPkgParam = Convert.ToInt32(Dts.Variables
["$Package::IntPkgParam"].Value);
string stringPkgParam = Dts.Variables["$Package::
StringPkgParam"].Value.ToString();
int intProjParam = Convert.ToInt32(Dts.Variables
["$Project::IntProjParam"].Value);
string stringProjParam = Dts.Variables["$Project::
StringProjParam"].Value.ToString();

string msg = "Table Count: " + tableCount.ToString();
Dts.Events.FireInformation(1001, subComponent,
msg, "", 0, ref fireAgain);

msg = "Package Parameters: IntPkgParam = " +
intPkgParam.ToString() + " ; StringPkgParam = " +
stringPkgParam;
Dts.Events.FireInformation(1001, subComponent, msg,
"", 0, ref fireAgain);

msg = "Project Parameters: IntProjParam = " +
intProjParam.ToString() + " ; StringProjParam = " +
stringProjParam;
Dts.Events.FireInformation(1001, subComponent,
msg, "", 0, ref fireAgain);

Dts.TaskResult = (int)ScriptResults.Success;
}
```

When completed the code in your VSTA Editor should appear similar to that shown in Figure 2-10.

```
public void Main()
{
    string packageName = Dts.Variables["System::PackageName"].Value.ToString();
    string taskName = Dts.Variables["System::TaskName"].Value.ToString();
    string subComponent = packageName + "." + taskName;
    bool fireAgain = true;

    int tableCount = Convert.ToInt32(Dts.Variables["User::TableCount"].Value);
    int intPkgParam = Convert.ToInt32(Dts.Variables["$Package::IntPkgParam"].Value);
    string stringPkgParam = Dts.Variables["$Package::StringPkgParam"].Value.ToString();
    int intProjParam = Convert.ToInt32(Dts.Variables["$Project::IntProjParam"].Value);
    string stringProjParam = Dts.Variables["$Project::StringProjParam"].Value.ToString();

    string msg = "Table Count: " + tableCount.ToString();
    Dts.Events.FireInformation(1001, subComponent, msg, "", 0, ref fireAgain);

    msg = "Package Parameters: IntPkgParam = " + intPkgParam.ToString() + " ; StringPkgParam = " + stringPkgParam;
    Dts.Events.FireInformation(1001, subComponent, msg, "", 0, ref fireAgain);

    msg = "Project Parameters: IntProjParam = " + intProjParam.ToString() + " ; StringProjParam = " + stringProjParam;
    Dts.Events.FireInformation(1001, subComponent, msg, "", 0, ref fireAgain);

    Dts.TaskResult = (int)ScriptResults.Success;
}
```

Figure 2-10. *Code in Your VSTA Editor*

Testing .Net Code Compiles Before Closing the VSTA Editor

Have you ever coded away in an SSIS Script task, only to close the VSTA Editor and then close the Script Task Editor to see the error shown in Figure 2-11?

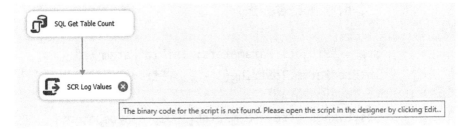

Figure 2-11. *Script task error in VSTA .Net code*

Kevin Hazzard shared a handy way to test the viability of the .Net code contained in the VSTA Editor *before* closing the editor. Click Build ➤ Build ST_... (VSTA scripts are uniquely named), as shown in Figure 2-12.

Figure 2-12. *Preparing to build a VSTA script*

When you click Build ST_..., the VSTA Editor attempts to build the script. In the lower left corner of the screen you will see "Build started," as shown in Figure 2-13.

Figure 2-13. *Build started*

If there is a bug in the .Net code, the build will fail. If there are no bugs in the .Net code, the build will succeed, as shown in Figure 2-14.

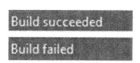

Figure 2-14. *Build succeeds or fails*

21

Close the VSTA Editor and click the OK button in the Script Task Editor. SimplePackage.dtsx should now appear as shown in Figure 2-15.

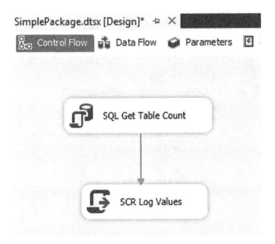

Figure 2-15. *SimplePackage.dtsx*

The demonstration SSIS package and project are complete.

Testing Progress

"All software is tested. Some intentionally."

– Andy Leonard, circa 2005

It's a good idea to always execute your package in the SSIS debugger. How else will you know that what you built works?

Press the F5 key to start the SSIS debugger. If all goes as planned, you should see both tasks succeed, as shown in Figure 2-16.

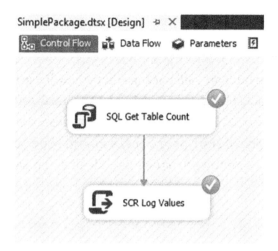

Figure 2-16. *Success!*

If you click the Progress tab, you should see the OnInformation messages raised by your script, as shown in Figure 2-17.

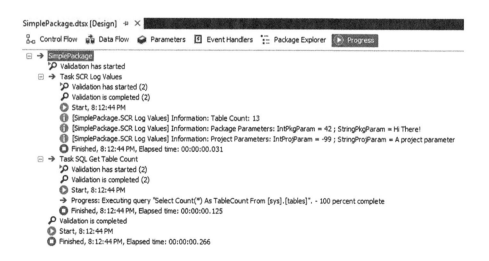

Figure 2-17. *OnInformation messages*

Your demo is now ready to begin an epic journey into data integration lifecycle management.

Conclusion

In this chapter, you built an SSIS package that you will use for the lessons throughout this book. I discussed data integration instrumentation and messaging to surface SSIS package execution log messages. It's important for us on the Dev side of DevOps to signal supporting personnel on the Ops side. It takes minutes to write this code that may save hours of troubleshooting.

CHAPTER 3

Source Control

Later in this book, I will discuss why SQL Server database backup and restore of the SSISDB database is not a viable method of SSIS code promotion. You should back up the SSISDB database just like you should back up all databases. You should not back up the SSISDB database for code promotion, and you should not back up the SSISDB database in lieu of source control.

There are two types of developers: those who use source control and those who will. People ask me, "Which source control engine is best, Andy?" My response is, "The one that you use." Please use source control.

This section is not an exhaustive tutorial on source control or using Team Foundation Services. I do not advocate one source control engine over another.

In this chapter, I will demonstrate using Team Foundation Services via Visual Studio Online (visualstudio.com). I will use the terms "source control" and "version control" interchangeably because modern source control engines also manage software versions.

© Andy Leonard 2018
A. Leonard, *Data Integration Life Cycle Management with SSIS*,
https://doi.org/10.1007/978-1-4842-3276-7_3

Source Control Client

Depending on which source control (or version control) engine you desire to use, you may or may not require a Visual Studio plug-in (or extension). Many developers use Subversion, a popular open-source version control system, with Tortoise SVN, a Subversion client implemented as a Windows shell. Tortoise is a highly intuitive interface that integrates into Windows Explorer to provide context-sensitive menus available by right-clicking file system folders that contain project artifacts under Subversion source control.

Git is a popular version control system created by Linus Torvalds (the creator of Linux). Git is a distributed source control system, which means each developer maintains a local working copy of the repository. Git relies heavily on *branching* (making another - usually local - copy of the current version of the code) and *merging* (the process of adding changes to the - usually local - edited version into another version of the code).

In this chapter I use Team Explorer, the Visual Studio plug-in for Team Foundation Services (TFS). You can learn more about Visual Studio plug-ins for TFS at `visualstudio.com/en-us/docs/tools`.

Creating a Team Project

In this section, I demonstrate how I use the free source control available at Visual Studio Online. I like Visual Studio Online because it's difficult to beat the price (free) and the total cost of ownership (also free). After setting up an account you can create a New Team Project from the dashboard. Mine is shown in Figure 3-1.

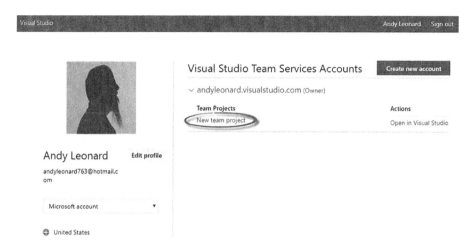

Figure 3-1. *Preparing to create a new team project*

You can think of Visual Studio Online source control as an extension of the Visual paradigm. The red box in Figure 3-2 is drawn around an SSIS package, which can be considered a Visual Studio *project artifact*. Project artifacts are lowest in the hierarchy of Visual Studio objects. The next level is the *project*, surrounded by a blue box in Figure 3-2. Visual Studio projects contain one or more project artifacts. Visual Studio *solutions*, such as the DILMSuite solution circled in green in Figure 3-2, contain one or more projects.

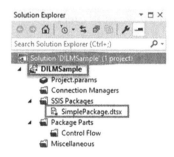

Figure 3-2. *The Visual Studio paradigm*

Team Foundation Server extends this paradigm an additional level: TFS *team projects* contain one or more Visual Studio solutions.

Click the "Create team project" link to proceed to the Create New Project page, shown in Figure 3-3.

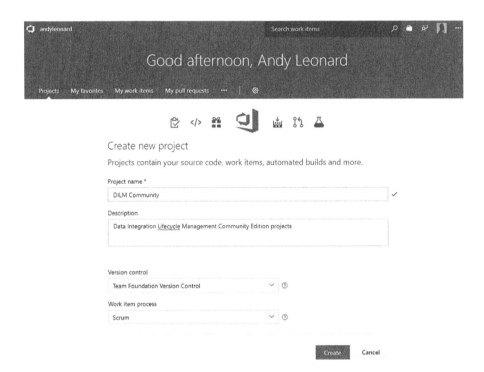

Figure 3-3.   *Creating a new team project*

To configure the new team project, add a name and optional description, and then select a version control engine (Team Foundation Version Control or Git) and a work item process. Click the Create button to create the team project and proceed to the Team Project page, as shown in Figure 3-4.

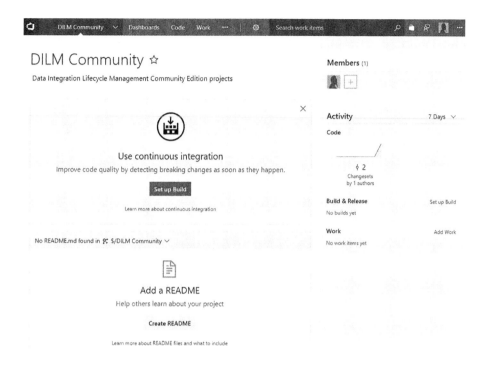

Figure 3-4. *New team project*

A new team project is now ready to go.

Configuring SSDT to Use TFS Online

Returning to SSDT, you next configure a connection to TFS Online. Begin by clicking the Team dropdown and clicking Manage Connections, as shown in Figure 3-5.

Figure 3-5. *Managing source control connections*

If you haven't configured a connection already, you may first see the Connect to Team Foundation Server window shown in Figure 3-6.

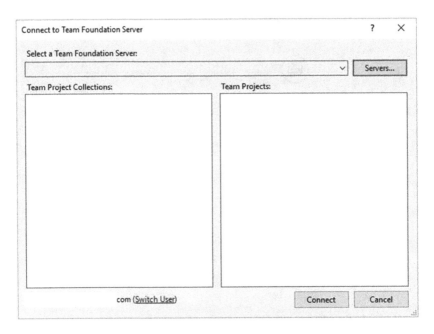

Figure 3-6. *Connecting to Team Foundation Server*

Click the Servers button to open the Add/Remove Team Foundation Server dialog, as shown in Figure 3-7.

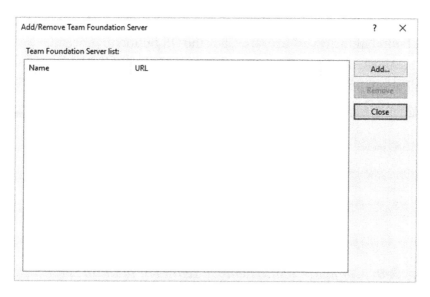

Figure 3-7. *Add/Remove Team Foundation Server*

Click the Add button to open the Add Team Foundation Server dialog, as shown in Figure 3-8.

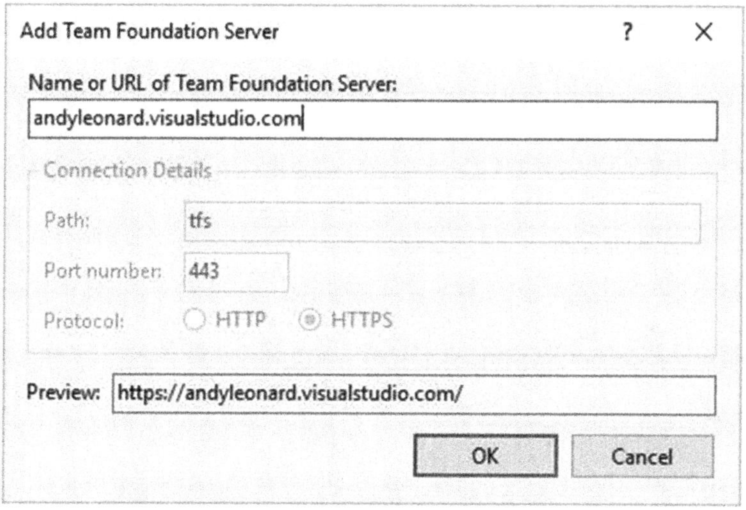

Figure 3-8. *Adding a Team Foundation Server*

Enter the URL of your TFS Online account page in the "Name or URL of Team Foundation Server" textbox. Click the OK button to proceed.

The Add Team Foundation Server dialog closes and the Add/Remove Team Foundation Server dialog should now list your TFS Online configuration and appear similar to that shown in Figure 3-9.

Figure 3-9. *Configured Add/Remove Team Foundation Server dialog*

Click the Close button to return to the Connect to Team Foundation Server dialog.

When the Connect to Team Foundation Server dialog displays, select your new team project, as shown in Figure 3-10.

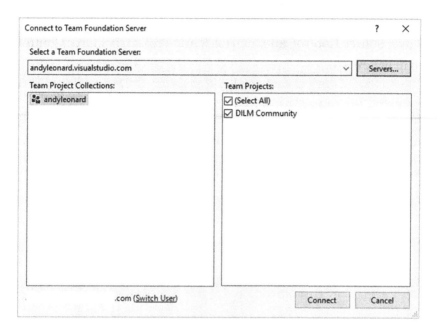

Figure 3-10. *Selecting a team project*

Click the Connect button. The Connect page of Team Explorer should now appear, similar to that shown in Figure 3-11.

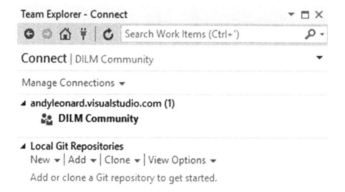

Figure 3-11. *Team Explorer connected to TFS Online*

In Solution Explorer, right-click the project name (DILMSample), hover over Source Control, and then click Add Project to Source Control, as shown in Figure 3-12.

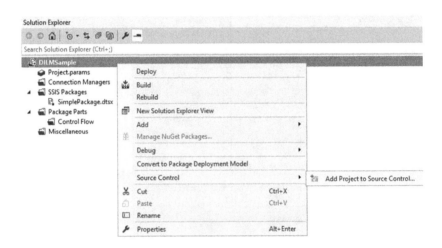

Figure 3-12.   *Preparing to add the project to source control*

The Add Solution <*Solution Name*> to Source Control dialog displays and contains the name of your team project in the team Project Locations listbox, as shown in Figure 3-13.

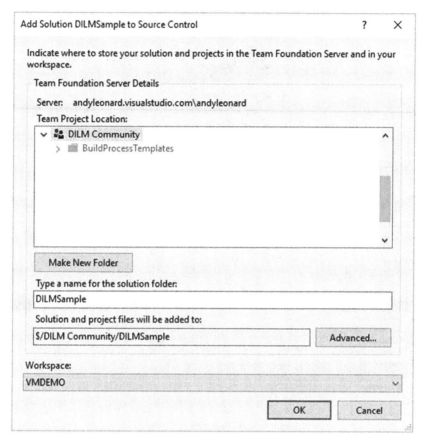

Figure 3-13. *Adding a solution to source control*

Click the OK button to add the DILMSample project to source control.

Once added, the solution artifacts are decorated with + symbols in Solution Explorer. The + symbol indicates the file is "newly added" to source control but not yet checked in, as shown in Figure 3-14.

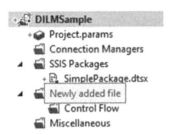

Figure 3-14. *Newly added to source control*

Check in the solution by right-clicking the project name, hovering over Source Control, and clicking Check In, as shown in Figure 3-15.

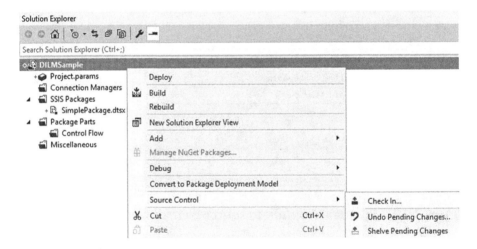

Figure 3-15. *Checking in the solution*

The Team Explorer Pending Changes window displays. It is a best practice to always add a version comment, as shown in Figure 3-16.

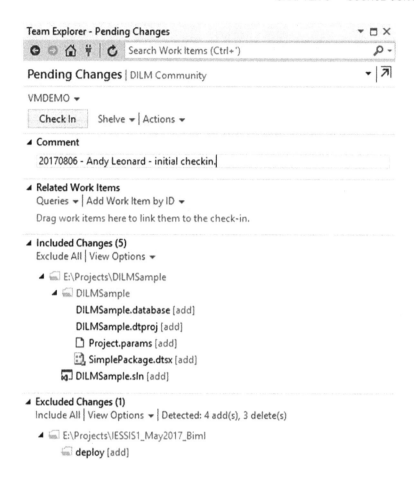

Figure 3-16. *Preparing to check in the project*

You may or may not be prompted to confirm the check-in, as shown in Figure 3-17.

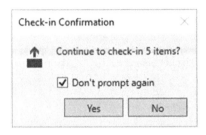

Figure 3-17. *Check-in confirmation*

Once checked in, Team Explorer's Pending Changes page will appear as shown in Figure 3-18.

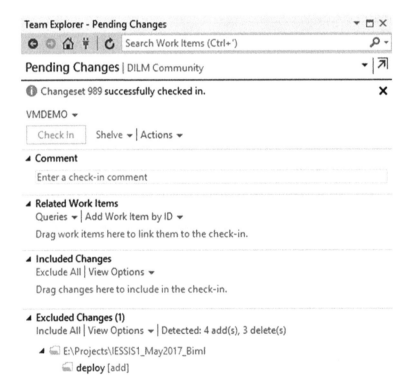

Figure 3-18. *All checked in*

Once checked in, Solution Explorer will display lock decorations beside checked-in artifacts, as shown in Figure 3-19.

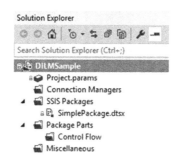

Figure 3-19. *Checked-in solution artifacts*

In this chapter, I demonstrated how to use Team Foundation Services (TFS) Online via the Visual Studio Online website. For more information, please visit visualstudio.com.

CHAPTER 4

Deploy to the SSIS Catalog

The SSIS catalog was released with SSIS 2012. Each release of SSIS since 2012 has featured upgrades to catalog functionality. There are several ways to deploy an SSIS project to the SSIS catalog. In this chapter, I will present two deployment options:

- Deploy from SSDT

- Deploy from an ISPAC file

A key tenet of DevOps is automation, and in this chapter I will discuss and demonstrate automated SSIS deployments.

Deploying from SSDT

Since the first release of the SSIS catalog, SSIS has been backwards-compatible. Prior to 2012, the deployment model for SSIS had no name; there was only one way to deploy SSIS and three targets: the file system, the MSDB database, and the "SSIS Package Store" (which was, by default, one folder in the file system and the MSDB database combined). Deployment to the SSIS catalog is a new way to deploy SSIS packages, so we needed a name for the "old way" as well as a name for the "new way." The new way

© Andy Leonard 2018
A. Leonard, *Data Integration Life Cycle Management with SSIS*,
https://doi.org/10.1007/978-1-4842-3276-7_4

is called "project deployment model" and the old way is called "package deployment model."

In this chapter (and book), I focus on the project deployment model. The project deployment model is required to deploy SSIS packages to the SSIS catalog.

To deploy your demo project, open the project in SSDT, right-click the project name in Solution Explorer, and click Deploy, as shown in Figure 4-1.

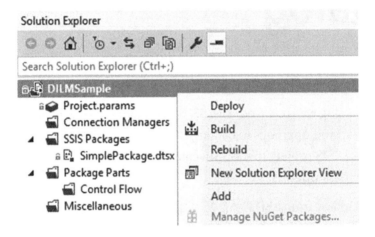

Figure 4-1. *Deploying the DILMSuite SSIS project from SSDT*

The Integration Services Deployment Wizard is an *extremely* functional piece of software. The underlying executable, ISDeploymentWizard.exe, sports a graphical user interface (GUI) *and* a command-line interface (CLI). The utility supports deployment from ISPAC file to SSIS catalog as well as SSIS catalog to SSIS catalog and, starting with SSIS 2016, supports package deployment as well as project deployment. I won't dive deeply into this awesome application; just know that I truly appreciate the excellence apparent in the Integration Services Deployment Wizard.

The Integration Services Deployment Wizard displays the Introduction page or the Select Destination page (if you previously checked the "Do not show this page again" checkbox on the Introduction page), as shown in Figure 4-2.

Figure 4-2. *The Integration Services Deployment Wizard Introduction page*

If the Introduction page is displayed, click the Next button to proceed to the Select Destination page.

Did I skip over the Select Source page? Yes. When started from inside SSDT, the Integration Services Deployment Wizard already has the information it needs about the source.

Enter the name of server that hosts your SSIS catalog. Click the Browse button to select the target catalog folder. When completed your Select Destination page should appear similar to that shown in Figure 4-3.

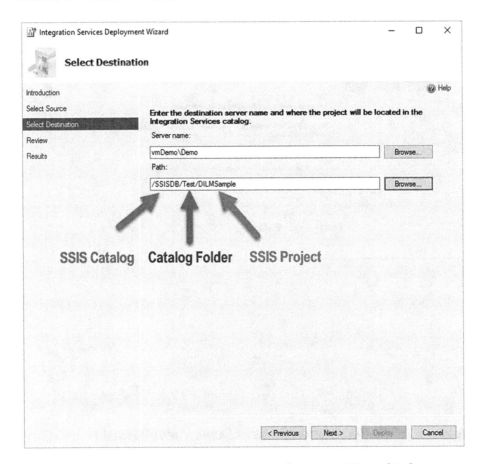

Figure 4-3. The Integration Services Deployment Wizard Select Destination page

The Path value shown on the Select Destination page refers to the SSIS catalog path of the SSIS project. SSIS catalog projects are contained in an SSIS catalog folder, which is contained in an SSIS catalog (which is always named SSISDB). SSIS packages are contained in SSIS catalog projects.

Click the Next button to proceed to the Review page, as shown in Figure 4-4.

Figure 4-4. *Reviewing deployment selections and options*

It's easy to skip right past the Integration Services Deployment Wizard Review page without giving it a second glance, but I want you to pause here with me for a moment because there is some information here that may prove useful to you in the future (or present).

Deploying from the Command Line

Deployment via CLI is powerful and useful for DevOps automation. The Source and Destination information is self-explanatory. Please note in the screenshot that I right-clicked the Command line to surface a context menu with a single option: Copy. I've pasted the command line here:

```
Command line: /Silent /ModelType:Project /SourcePath:"E:\
Projects\DILMSample\DILMSample\bin\Development\DILMSample.
ispac" /DestinationServer:"vmDemo\Demo" /DestinationPath:
"/SSISDB/Test/DILMSample"
```

SSIS ships with a number of utilities, some of which may be called from a command prompt. Any utility that can be called from a command prompt may be scheduled using SQL Agent (provided command-line execution is enabled), Windows Scheduler, or almost any other scheduling service or utility.

In order to use the command line shared on the Integration Services Deployment Wizard Review page, you need to know a couple things:

1. The location of the executable

2. The meaning of the switches and values

I installed the Demo instance of SQL Server on vmDemo's E: drive so the location of ISDeploymentWizard.exe is E:\Program Files\Microsoft SQL Server\130\DTS\Binn\ISDeploymentWizard.exe, as shown in Figure 4-5.

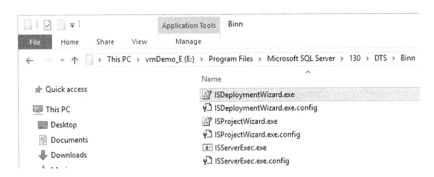

Figure 4-5. *The location of the ISDeploymentWizard.exe file*

This is the same application that is currently open and executing; it is the Integration Services Deployment Wizard executable. As mentioned earlier, the executable exposes two interfaces: a GUI and a CLI. It's possible to execute the entire deployment of your SSIS project, DILMSuite, by opening a command prompt, supplying the path to ISDeploymentWizard. exe followed by the command line above. Don't believe me? Check out Figure 4-6.

Figure 4-6. *Deployment via the command line*

There's good news and bad news here. The good news is this execution succeeded. The bad news? There is no feedback provided if the execution succeeds. How can you tell it succeeded? Well, it didn't fail. What does a failure look like? A failure may result in a prompt from the CLI that gives you a list of the acceptable switches, as shown in Figure 4-7.

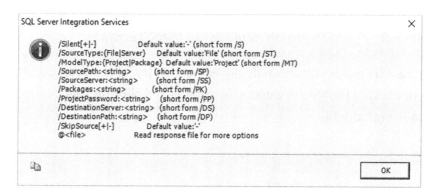

Figure 4-7. *Deployment failure using the CLI*

This isn't the only failure response. For example, if you mistype the name of the destination server, you will get a "Failed to connect" message after ISDeploymentWizard.exe tries to contact the server for 30 seconds. That message will appear similar to Figure 4-8.

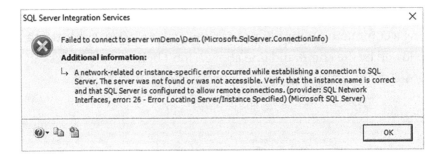

Figure 4-8. *Deployment failure due to connection error*

Another way to detect success is to use SSMS to connect to the SSIS catalog and check for the existence of your SSIS project, as shown in Figure 4-9.

Figure 4-9. *The SSIS project deployed to the SSIS catalog*

If the SSIS project has been deployed before, though, you can check by right-clicking the SSIS project in the catalog and clicking Versions, as shown in Figure 4-10.

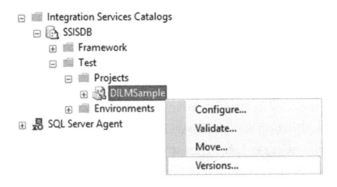

Figure 4-10. *Opening SSIS catalog project versions*

The Project Versions dialog displays as shown in Figure 4-11.

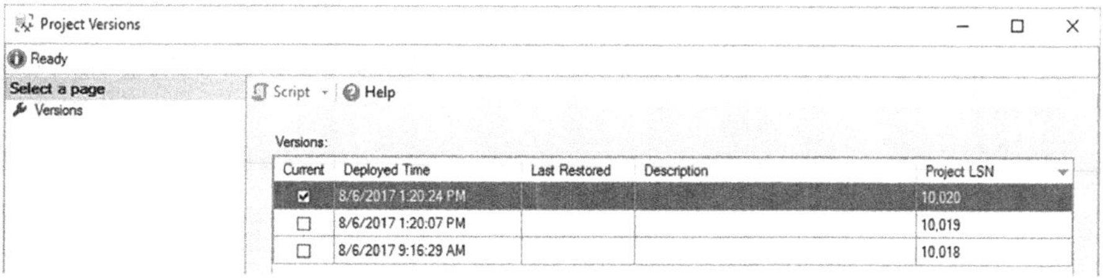

Figure 4-11. *Viewing SSIS catalog project versions*

The last deployment is marked as Current.

Returning to your deployment from SSDT, if you click the Deploy button on the Integration Services Deployment Wizard Review page, the Deployment Wizard will attempt to deploy your SSIS project to the SSIS catalog you selected, into the SSIS catalog folder you specified, as shown in Figure 4-12.

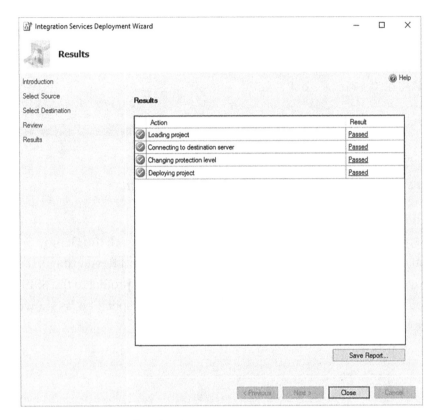

Figure 4-12. Successful deployment

If all goes as hoped, the deployment will be a success.

Deployment Failures

Sometimes bad things happen to good deployments. You may be reading this book because you experienced a deployment failure triggered by a good-faith effort to restore the SSIS catalog database, SSISDB.

Backup and restore is not a recommended method for promoting or transferring SSIS projects between SSIS catalogs!

When you attempt to deploy an SSIS project (or package) to an SSIS catalog after SSISDB was improperly restored, the deployment will *not* succeed. Instead, your Integration Services Deployment Wizard Results page will appear as shown in Figure 4-13.

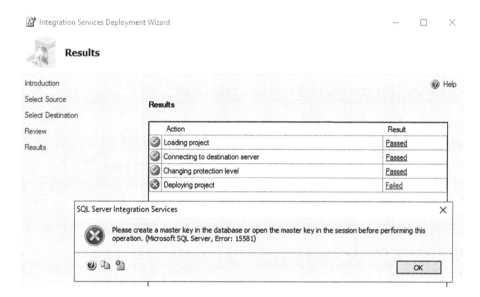

Figure 4-13. *Failed SSIS project deployment*

When you click the Failed link, the message box in Figure 4-13 will display the error message,

> Please create a master key in the database or open the master key in the session before performing this operation. (Microsoft SQL Server, Error: 15581)

Please find more information about backing up and restoring the SSIS catalog database (SSISDB) on the SSIS Catalog page in the section titled "Back up, Restore, and Move the SSIS Catalog" (docs.microsoft.com/en-us/sql/integration-services/service/ssis-catalog). I blogged about this scenario and the post includes a script one can use to restore SSISDB. You can find my post titled "Deploying SSIS Projects to a Restored

51

SSIS Catalog" at andyleonard.blog/2017/07/29/deploying-ssis-projects-to-a-restored-ssis-catalog-ssisdb. The script I use is the following:

```
/*

  My script for restoring SSISDB to a SQL Server 2016 SP1
instance of SQL Server.
I followed the instructions found at https://msdn.microsoft.
com/en-us/library/hh213291(v=sql.130).aspx

Hope this helps,
Andy Leonard
*** Action is required where you see three asterisks "***"

*/

-- create the ##MS_SSISServerCleanupJobLogin## login if it does
not already exist.
USE [master]
GO

print '##MS_SSISServerCleanupJobLogin## login'
If Not Exists(Select [name]
From sys.sql_logins
Where [name] = '##MS_SSISServerCleanupJobLogin##')
begin
print ' - Creating the ##MS_SSISServerCleanupJobLogin## login'
CREATE LOGIN [##MS_SSISServerCleanupJobLogin##] WITH PASSWORD
=N'DWehrJfiRgMxEFaE=KxomUkF7fnV3poW/ZQPJ' -- *** change this,
please - Andy
, DEFAULT_DATABASE=[master]
, DEFAULT_LANGUAGE=[us_english]
, CHECK_EXPIRATION=OFF
, CHECK_POLICY=OFF
```

```
print ' - ##MS_SSISServerCleanupJobLogin## login created'
end
Else
print ' - ##MS_SSISServerCleanupJobLogin## already exists.'
GO

print ''

print ' - Disabling the ##MS_SSISServerCleanupJobLogin## login'
ALTER LOGIN [##MS_SSISServerCleanupJobLogin##] DISABLE
print ' - ##MS_SSISServerCleanupJobLogin## login disabled'
GO

USE [master]
GO

SET ANSI_NULLS ON
GO

SET QUOTED_IDENTIFIER ON
GO

print 'dbo.sp_ssis_startup stored procedure'
If Exists(Select s.name + '.' + p.name
From sys.procedures p
Join sys.schemas s
On s.[schema_id] = p.[schema_id]
Where s.[name] = 'dbo'
And p.name = 'sp_ssis_startup')
begin
print ' - Dropping dbo.sp_ssis_startup stored procedure'
Drop PROCEDURE [dbo].[sp_ssis_startup]
print ' - dbo.sp_ssis_startup stored procedure dropped'
end
```

```
print ' - Creating dbo.sp_ssis_startup stored procedure'
go

    CREATE PROCEDURE [dbo].[sp_ssis_startup]
AS
SET NOCOUNT ON
/* Currently, the IS Store name is 'SSISDB' */
IF DB_ID('SSISDB') IS NULL
RETURN

IF NOT EXISTS(SELECT name FROM [SSISDB].sys.procedures WHERE
name=N'startup')
RETURN

/*Invoke the procedure in SSISDB  */
/* Use dynamic sql to handle AlwaysOn non-readable mode*/
DECLARE @script nvarchar(500)
SET @script = N'EXEC [SSISDB].[catalog].[startup]'
EXECUTE sp_executesql @script
GO
print ' - dbo.sp_ssis_startup stored procedure created'
print ''

use master
go
print 'Enabling SQLCLR'
exec sp_configure 'clr enabled', 1
reconfigure
print 'SQLCLR enabled'
print ''

print 'MS_SQLEnableSystemAssemblyLoadingKey asymetric key'
If Not Exists(Select [name]
From sys.asymmetric_keys
```

```
Where [name] = 'MS_SQLEnableSystemAssemblyLoadingKey')
begin
print ' - Creating MS_SQLEnableSystemAssemblyLoadingKey'
Create Asymmetric key MS_SQLEnableSystemAssemblyLoadingKey
From Executable File = 'E:\Program Files\Microsoft SQL
Server\130\DTS\Binn\Microsoft.SqlServer.IntegrationServices.
Server.dll'  -- *** check this, please - Andy
print ' - MS_SQLEnableSystemAssemblyLoadingKey created'
end
Else
print ' - MS_SQLEnableSystemAssemblyLoadingKey already exists.'
go
print ''

print 'MS_SQLEnableSystemAssemblyLoadingUser SQL Login'
If Not Exists(Select [name]
From sys.sql_logins
Where [name] = 'MS_SQLEnableSystemAssemblyLoadingUser')
begin
print ' - Attempting to create MS_
SQLEnableSystemAssemblyLoadingUser Sql login'
begin try
Create Login MS_SQLEnableSystemAssemblyLoadingUser
From Asymmetric key MS_SQLEnableSystemAssemblyLoadingKey
print ' - MS_SQLEnableSystemAssemblyLoadingUser Sql login
created'
print ' - Granting Unsafe Assembly permission to MS_SQL
EnableSystemAssemblyLoadingUser'
Grant unsafe Assembly to MS_SQLEnableSystemAssemblyLoadingUser
print ' - MS_SQLEnableSystemAssemblyLoadingUser granted Unsafe
Assembly permission'
end try
```

```
begin catch
print ' - Something went wrong while attempting to create the
MS_SQLEnableSystemAssemblyLoadingUser Sql login, but it''s
probably ok...'
-- nothing for now
end catch
end
Else
print ' - MS_SQLEnableSystemAssemblyLoadingUser Sql login
already exists.'

go

print ''

print 'Restoring SSISDB'
USE [master]

begin try
ALTER DATABASE [SSISDB] SET SINGLE_USER WITH ROLLBACK IMMEDIATE
end try
begin catch
-- ignore the error (usually happens because the database
doesn't exist...)
end catch

RESTORE DATABASE [SSISDB]
FROM DISK = N'E:\Andy\backup\SSISDB_SP1.bak'  -- *** check
this, please - Andy
WITH FILE = 1,
MOVE N'data' To N'E:\Program Files\Microsoft SQL Server\
MSSQL13.TEST\MSSQL\DATA\SSISDB.mdf',   -- *** check this,
please - Andy
```

```
MOVE N'log' TO N'E:\Program Files\Microsoft SQL Server\MSSQL13.
TEST\MSSQL\DATA\SSISDB.ldf',    -- *** check this, please - Andy
NOUNLOAD
, REPLACE
, STATS = 5

ALTER DATABASE [SSISDB] SET MULTI_USER

GO
print ' - SSISDB restore complete'
print ''

print 'Set ProcOption to 1 for dbo.sp_ssis_startup stored
procedure'
EXEC sp_procoption N'[dbo].[sp_ssis_startup]', 'startup', '1'
print 'ProcOption set to 1 for dbo.sp_ssis_startup stored
procedure'

GO
print ''

Use SSISDB
go

print '##MS_SSISServerCleanupJobUser## user in SSISDB database'
If Not Exists(Select *
From sys.sysusers
Where [name] = '##MS_SSISServerCleanupJobUser##')
begin
print ' - Creating ##MS_SSISServerCleanupJobUser## user'
CREATE USER [##MS_SSISServerCleanupJobUser##] FOR LOGIN
[##MS_SSISServerCleanupJobLogin##] WITH DEFAULT_SCHEMA=[dbo]
print ' - ##MS_SSISServerCleanupJobUser## user created'
end
```

```
Else
print ' - ##MS_SSISServerCleanupJobUser## already exists.'
GO
print ''

/*

-- One method for restoring the master key from the file.
-- NOTE: You must have the original SSISDB encryption password!

Restore master key from file = 'E:\Andy\backup\SSISDB_SP1_
key'    -- *** check this, please - Andy
Decryption by password = 'SuperSecretPassword' -- 'Password
used to encrypt the master key during SSISDB backup'    -- ***
check this, please - Andy
Encryption by password = 'SuperSecretPassword' -- 'New
Password'    -- *** check this, please - Andy
Force
go
*/

-- Another method for restoring the master key from the file.
-- NOTE: You must have the original SSISDB encryption password!
print 'Opening the master key'
Open master key decryption by password = 'SuperSecretPassword'
--'Password used when creating SSISDB'    -- *** check this,
please - Andy
Alter Master Key
Add encryption by Service Master Key
go
print 'Master key opened'

print ''

print 'Checking the SSIS Catalog Schema Version'
exec [catalog].check_schema_version @use32bitruntime = 0
```

58

The Transact-SQL script listed above requires you to supply the password used to create the SSIS catalog; replace the text "SuperSecretPassword" with the password for your SSIS catalog. Each place you see the comment, `-- *** check this, please - Andy`, please check the preceding line of T-SQL.

Conclusion

In this chapter, I demonstrated deploying an SSIS project to the SSIS catalog. You examined the Integration Services Deployment Wizard's GUI and CLI. I discussed the importance of deployment in any enterprise that practices DevOps.

CHAPTER 5

Configure the SSIS Catalog Project

A key tenet of enterprise DevOps is *externalization*, which is the configuration or parameterization of code. The configuration is stored apart from the code itself. Externalization promotes code reuse and supports decoupling, both best practices in software development. In this chapter, I focus on externalizing SSIS connection manager connection string properties because I believe it is an SSIS best practice to manage SSIS project and package connection strings via external configurations.

Your DILMSample SSIS project is deployed to your SSIS catalog. Expanding the Integration Services Catalogs node in SSMS's Object Explorer surfaces the view shown in Figure 5-1.

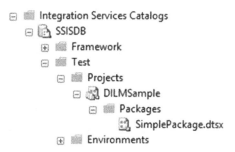

Figure 5-1. *The DILMSample SSIS project in the Integration Services Catalogs node, as shown by SSMS's Object Explorer*

© Andy Leonard 2018
A. Leonard, *Data Integration Life Cycle Management with SSIS*,
https://doi.org/10.1007/978-1-4842-3276-7_5

You see the SSIS catalog (SSISDB), two SSIS catalog folders (Framework and Test), one SSIS catalog project in the Test catalog folder (DILMSample), and one SSIS package in the DILMSample catalog project (SimplePackage.dtsx).

Why do I write *SSIS project* in some places and *SSIS catalog project* in other places? I am referring to two distinct objects.

1. An SSIS project exists in the context of SQL Server Development Tools (SSDT). It is a (hopefully source-controlled) project under development.

2. An SSIS catalog project is an SSIS project that has been deployed to an SSIS catalog.

It will help to think of SSIS catalog projects as separate and distinct objects, separated from the SSIS projects that exist outside the SSIS catalog, especially when thinking of SSIS catalog project configuration. The two are weakly coupled in this fashion: changes made to the SSIS project may impact its related SSIS catalog project, and then only after deployment to the SSIS catalog. Changes made to the SSIS catalog project in no way impact the SSIS project.

Configuring Projects

You have several options for configuring your SSIS catalog project. In SSMS Object Explorer's Integration Services Catalogs node, expand the subnodes to the DILMSample project level. Right-click the DILMSample SSIS catalog project and click Configure, as shown in Figure 5-2.

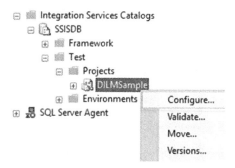

Figure 5-2. *Preparing to configure the DILMSample catalog project*

The Configure – DILMSample dialog opens.

Configuring Connections

The SSIS catalog treats connection manager properties like parameters. In fact, if you query the [catalog].[object_parameters] view, you will find parameters with names like "CM.*<SSIS Connection Manager Name>*. ConnectionString". This is a connection manager parameter. I'm pretty sure "CM" indicates "connection manager." "*<SSIS Connection Manager Name>*.ConnectionString" is a connection manager's ConnectionString property, for sure.

When the Configure – DILMSample window displays, click the Connection Managers tab to view the connection's configuration, as shown in Figure 5-3.

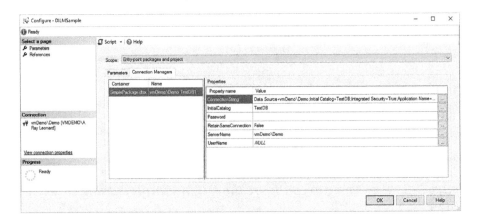

Figure 5-3. *Viewing the connection manager's configuration*

Note the listbox below the Parameters and Connection Managers tabs. It surfaces the container (a catalog project artifact) and name (of the connection manager). My SSIS project contains a single connection manager in SimplePackage.dtsx, so SimplePackage.dtsx is the container and the connection manager name is vmDemo\Demo.TestDB1. The name of your connection manager will almost certainly differ, as will your ConnectionString property, to which you next turn your attention.

The value in the ConnectionString property is the value configured at design time. The SSIS catalog will always have access to design-time default values. If I execute the SimplePackage.dtsx SSIS package in the SSIS catalog as it is currently configured, it will execute and attempt to connect to the vmDemo\Demo instance of SQL Server and the TestDB database. Because I've deployed this SSIS project to the SSIS catalog hosted on the vmDemo\Demo SQL Server instance, the SimplePackage.dtsx package should execute without issue.

But what happens when I deploy the DILMSample SSIS project to a *different* SSIS catalog? SimplePackage.dtsx may or may not execute successfully, depending on a number of factors that impact whether processes executing on one server can connect to SQL Server instances hosted on other servers.

One key thing to remember is this: as the SSIS project is configured at this time, each time I deploy the DILMSample SSIS project, the default value of the vmDemo\Demo.TestDB1 connection manager in SimplePackage.dtsx will *always* be configured to connect to the vmDemo\ Demo instance of SQL Server and the TestDB database on that instance.

Overriding the Connection Configuration

How does one change the connection configuration? Click the ellipsis to the right of the ConnectionString property's Value textbox, circled in Figure 5-4.

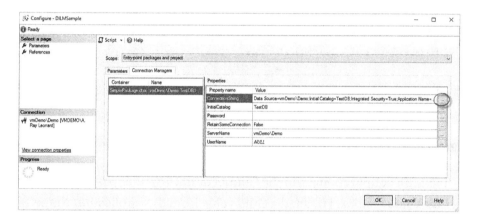

Figure 5-4. *Preparing to open the ConnectionString's Value configuration*

The Set Parameter Value dialog opens.

In the SSIS catalog, project parameters, package parameters, and connection manager properties are all considered parameters.

Select and copy the design-time default value of the ConnectionString property, found in the textbox beside the "Use default value from package" option, and paste it into the "Edit value" textbox, as shown in Figure 5-5.

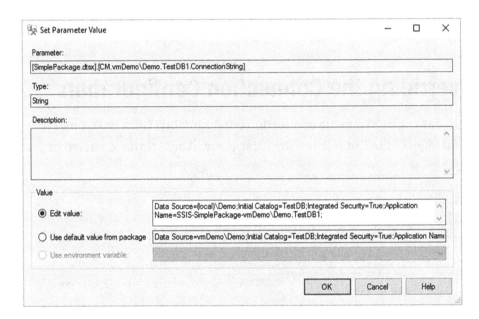

Figure 5-5. *Editing the ConnectionString property value*

I made a couple changes to the ConnectionString after pasting it into the Edit Value textbox. I deleted a Guid value from the Application Name setting and I changed the data source from vmDemo\Demo to (local)\Demo. The data source is technically the same as before. I made the change so that I can later be certain which value is being used: the design-time default or this *literal override.*

Click the OK button to proceed to the override page in Figure 5-6.

Figure 5-6. *A catalog project literal override*

The ConnectionString value has been overridden by an SSIS catalog literal override. This is indicated by the **bold text decoration** of the value. You can think of a literal override as hard-coding a configuration value into the SSIS catalog. Subsequent deployments of the DILMSample SSIS project to this SSIS catalog will *not* change the value of the literal override, even if you change the value of the connection manager's design-time default ConnectionString value. This is one reason I refer to an *SSIS project* in SSDT and an *SSIS catalog project* or *catalog project* once it has been deployed to an SSIS catalog.

As someone with permission to configure an SSIS catalog, you can always revert any literal override to the design-time default value by selecting the "Use default value from package" option in the Set Parameter Value dialog, as shown in Figure 5-7.

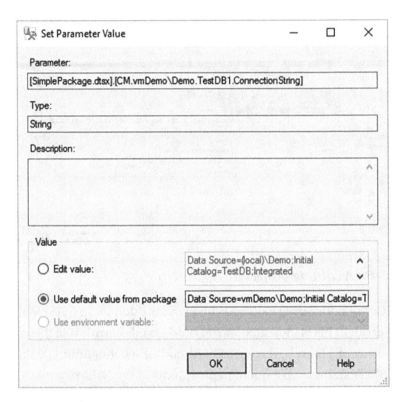

Figure 5-7. *Reselecting the design-time default*

The value text decoration returns to none and the value reverts to the design-time default, as shown in Figure 5-8.

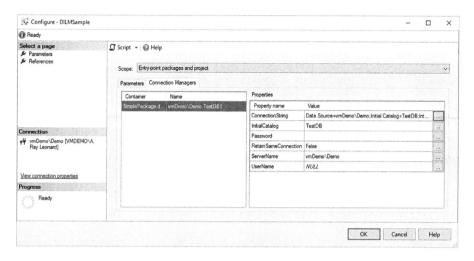

Figure 5-8. *Reverted to design-time default*

Externalizing the Connection Configuration

So far you've examined two sources of SSIS catalog project configurations settings: design-time defaults and literal overrides. You probably noticed a third option on the Set Parameter Values dialog, one that was disabled. "Use environment variable" is the third option but it requires additional configuration before this option is enabled.

Before we jump into the next demo, let's discuss how the SSIS catalog manages *externalization*. Externalization is storing values in some other location for use at runtime. The SSIS catalog's mechanism for externalization is SSIS catalog environments. Catalog environments contain a collection of catalog environment variables which, in turn, contain values that are used at runtime to override catalog project parameter values.

That last paragraph is relatively short for the depth and importance of the information contained therein. Please let it sink in before proceeding.

Let's talk about the SSIS catalog's externalization mechanism in more detail. Let's begin with an SSIS catalog environment, as shown in Figure 5-9.

Figure 5-9. *A catalog environment (figuratively)*

The SSIS catalog environment contains a collection of zero or more SSIS catalog environment variables, as shown in Figure 5-10.

Figure 5-10. *A catalog environment variable in a catalog environment*

To connect an SSIS catalog environment to an SSIS catalog project, the SSIS catalog uses a *reference*. A reference is simply a relationship that connects a catalog project to a catalog environment, as shown in Figure 5-11.

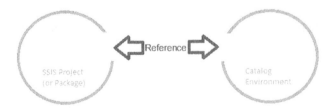

Figure 5-11. *A reference relating an SSIS catalog project to an SSIS catalog environment*

In order for a parameter in a catalog project to consume a catalog environment variable value, a *reference mapping* is created. A reference mapping maps a value stored in an SSIS catalog environment variable to a parameter in an SSIS catalog project, as shown in Figure 5-12.

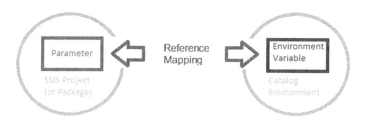

Figure 5-12. *A reference mapping between an SSIS catalog project parameter and an SSIS catalog environment variable*

To restate, because this can be a challenging topic, you first create and configure an SSIS catalog environment. Configuring the catalog environment includes defining SSIS catalog environment variables. That's the first step in externalization.

You next create a reference between an SSIS catalog environment and an SSIS catalog project. Creating a reference is the second step in externalization.

You may then assign SSIS catalog environment variables to SSIS catalog project parameters via the reference. This is reference mapping. Mapping a parameter value to a catalog environment variable value via a reference is the third step in externalization.

Let's walk through this procedure in a demo.

Creating an Environment

In the SSIS catalog, right-click the Environments virtual folder found in the Test catalog folder and then click Create Environment, as shown in Figure 5-13.

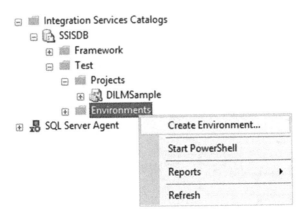

Figure 5-13. *Preparing to create a catalog environment*

When the Create Environment dialog displays, provide an environment name and optional description, as shown in Figure 5-14.

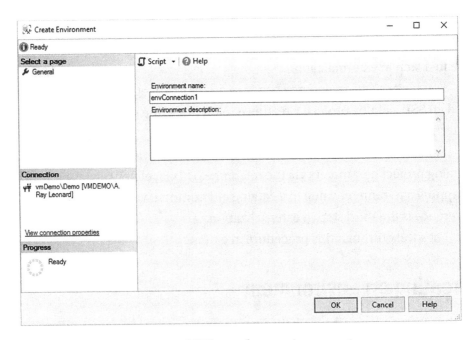

Figure 5-14. *Creating an SSIS catalog environment*

Click OK to close the Create Environment dialog.

Configuring an Environment

Expand the Environments virtual folder in the SSIS catalog. Right-click the new catalog environment and click Properties, as shown in Figure 5-15.

Figure 5-15. *Preparing to configure the SSIS catalog environment variables*

Click the Variables page. Add a name for your catalog environment variable (I named mine ConnectionString). Set the type to String. Add a valid connection string to the Value field, as shown in Figure 5-16.

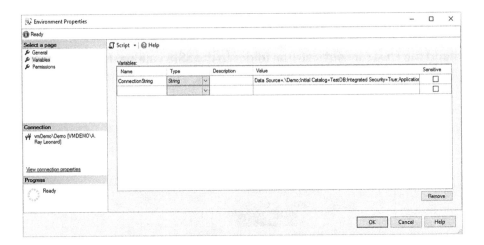

Figure 5-16. *Configuring an SSIS catalog environment variable*

Click the OK button to close the Environment Properties dialog.

Configuring a Reference

Right-click the DILMSample catalog project and click Configure. When the Configure – DILMSample dialog opens, click the References page. Click the Add button and select the catalog environment you just created beneath the Local Folder (Test) virtual folder in the Browse Environments dialog, as shown in Figure 5-17.

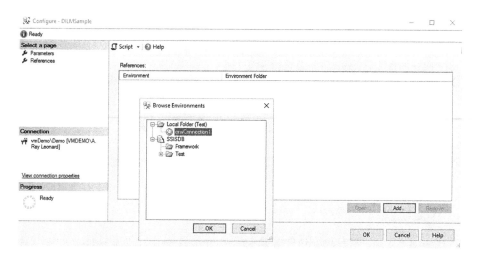

Figure 5-17. *Selecting the catalog environment for the reference*

There are actually two "paths" to the envConnection1 catalog environment available in the Browse Environments dialog. The `Local Folder` path creates a "relative" reference in SSIS catalog parlance. If you expand the SSISDB ➤ Test folder, you could select the *same* envConnection1 catalog environment. This would create an "absolute" reference.

Click the OK button to select the catalog environment for the reference. The Configure – DILMSample references page will appear similar to that shown in Figure 5-18.

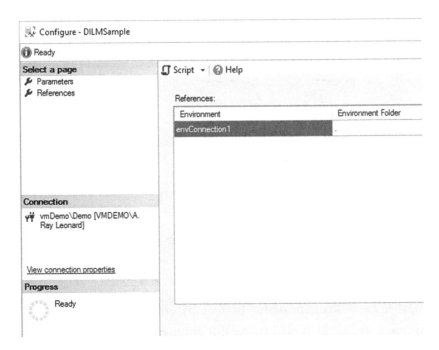

Figure 5-18. *Reference configured!*

Please note the "." in the Environment Folder column; it indicates you selected a local catalog environment, or a catalog environment from the *same* catalog folder as the catalog project.

Configuring a Reference Mapping

Click the Parameters page and then click the Connection Managers tab. Click the ellipsis beside the ConnectionString property for your lone connection manager to open the Set Parameter Value dialog. Please note all three value configuration options are now enabled. Select the "Use environment variable" option and then select the ConnectionString catalog environment variable from the dropdown, as shown in Figure 5-19.

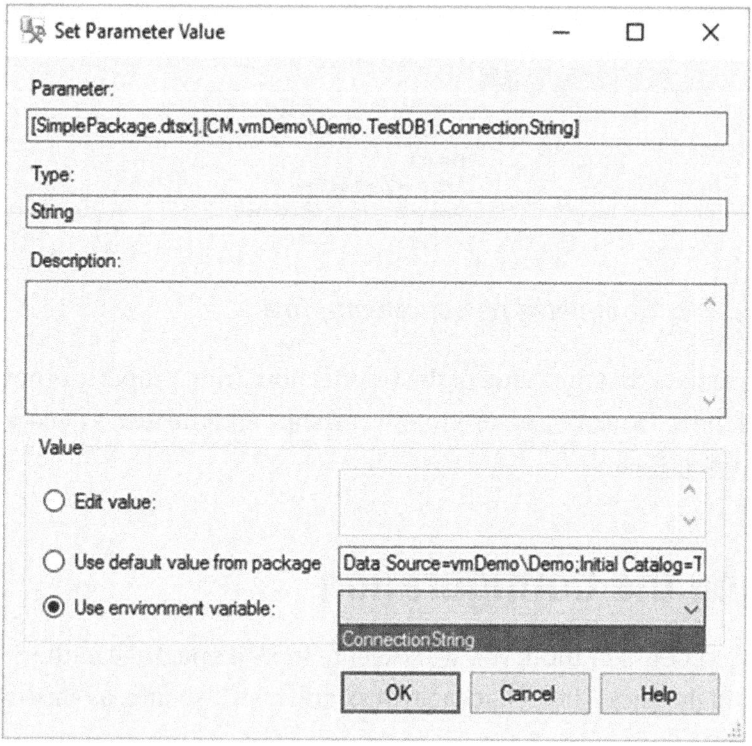

Figure 5-19. *Selecting the catalog environment variable for the reference mapping*

Click the OK button to create the reference mapping between the SSIS catalog project parameter, `SimplePackage.dtsx`'s `vmDemo\Demo\testDB1` connection manager ConnectionString, and the SSIS catalog environment variable named ConnectionString found in the reference to the SSIS catalog environment you created a few minutes ago. Your Configure – DILMSample dialog should now appear similar to that shown in Figure 5-20.

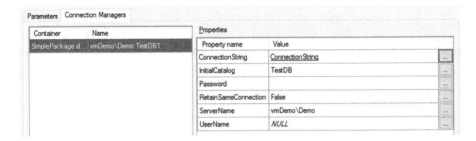

Figure 5-20. *Completed reference mapping!*

Please note that the value of the ConnectionString property is now the name of the SSIS catalog environment variable, and the text is decorated with an underline.

Testing the Configuration

To test your configuration, you will execute the SSIS package in the SSIS catalog. Right-click SimplePackage.dtsx and click Execute, as shown in Figure 5-21.

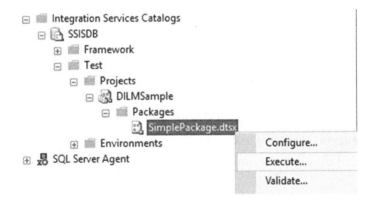

Figure 5-21. *Executing SimplePackage.dtsx*

You'll see an error message at the top of the Execute Package dialog when the Execute Package dialog displays. Click the error to see the error message displayed in a message box, as shown in Figure 5-22.

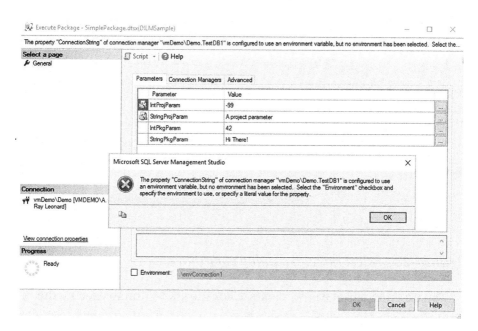

Figure 5-22. *Displaying the execute package error message*

To clear the error, follow the instructions included in the error message. Check the Environment checkbox and select an SSIS catalog environment from the dropdown, as shown in Figure 5-23.

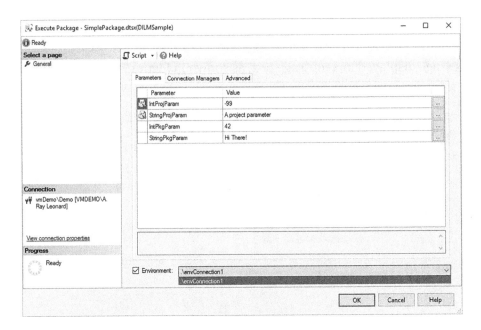

Figure 5-23. *Select an SSIS catalog environment*

The execute package error clears. Click the OK button to execute the SimplePackage.dtsx SSIS package. A message box similar to that shown in Figure 5-24 informs you that package execution has started and asks if you would like to view the Overview Report.

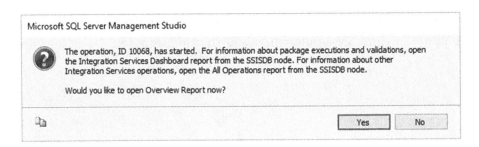

Figure 5-24. *Overview Report prompt*

Click the Yes button to display the Overview Report, shown in Figure 5-25.

Overview

on VMDEMO\DEMO at 8/8/2017 7:18:18 AM

This report provides an overview of the package tasks and parameters, including execution or validation information.

View Messages

View Performance

Execution Information

Operation ID	10068
Package	Test\DILMSample\SimplePackage.dtsx
Environment	\envConnection1
Status	Failed
Machine	VMDEMO

Duration (sec)	2.454
Start Time	8/8/2017 7:18:07 AM
End Time	8/8/2017 7:18:10 AM
Caller	VMDEMO\A. Ray Leonard

Execution Overview

Filter: Result: All: (3 more)

Result	Duration (sec)	Package Name	Task Name	Execution Path

No task information is available. One or more filters have been set, or one or more errors occurred during pre-execution. For information about the error messages, click View Messages to open the Messages report.

Parameters Used

Name	Value	Data Type
CALLER_INFO		String
DUMP_EVENT_CODE	0	String
DUMP_ON_ERROR	False	Boolean
DUMP_ON_EVENT	False	Boolean
IntPkgParam	42	Int32
IntProjParam	-99	Int32
LOGGING_LEVEL	1	Int32
StringPkgParam	Hi There!	String
StringProjParam	A project parameter	String
SYNCHRONIZED	False	Boolean
vmDemo\Demo.TestDB1.Connection String	Data Source=.\Demo;Initial Catalog=TestDB;Integrated Security=True;Application Name=SSIS-SimplePackage-TestDB;	String

Property Overrides

Property Path	Property Value

Figure 5-25. *The Overview Report*

Please note the value for the vmDemo\Demo.TestDB1.ConnectionString parameter. The value at runtime is the value of the ConnectionString catalog environment variable you configured in the catalog environment named envConnection1. This test verifies that the reference mapping is configured and working properly.

Conclusion

These are the three sources of values for SSIS parameters in the SSIS catalog (with matching text decoration):

1. Design-time defaults

2. **Literal overrides**

3. Reference mappings

Design-time defaults remain stored in the SSIS catalog but may be overridden using literal overrides or references and reference mappings to catalog environments and environment variables, respectively.

CHAPTER 6

Catalog Browser

I was honored to be a Microsoft SQL Server MVP for five years (2007-2012). One cool thing about being a Microsoft MVP was access to the internal developer teams. Everyone could file Microsoft Connect items to report bugs and make suggestions for product improvements. Many MVPs did so only to have their bug reports marked as "works as designed" or "won't fix" and suggestions responded to with something similar. It was discouraging. There are reasons many Connect items were addressed in this way. I am happy to report the root cause (performance-based management, or PBM) has been abandoned *and* the Microsoft Developer Teams are really and truly listening and responding to requests from the field.

Why I Built DILM Suite, by Andy Leonard

That doesn't mean every suggestion is acted upon (I promise this is not a complaint). It turns out that Microsoft is a software development enterprise. As big as Microsoft is, it can't possibly respond to *every* request. When I realized this, I began thinking about how I might address gaps I perceived. I'd cofounded a consulting company and we (collectively) weren't interested in becoming a software product company. But I was *very* interested in developing products to address gaps in data integration lifecycle management (DILM).

83

© Andy Leonard 2018
A. Leonard, *Data Integration Life Cycle Management with SSIS*,
https://doi.org/10.1007/978-1-4842-3276-7_6

In 2015 I left the consulting company I cofounded and immediately began developing the software I'd dreamed of building. In my opinion, the most fair answers to the question of "Why?" are the following:

1. I came to believe the Microsoft SSIS Developer Team would never address the things I perceived as "gaps" in the product story.

2. I came to believe that the consulting company I cofounded and I held irreconcilable visions of how to address DILM issues.

Looking back with two years of perspective, I believe focusing on DILM was the best long-term move for me. I started another consulting company, Enterprise Data & Analytics (entdna.com), mostly to fund my coding habit.

Surfacing the SSIS Catalog

Let's examine the SSIS catalog surface in the SSMS Object Explorer's Integration Services Catalogs node, shown in Figure 6-1.

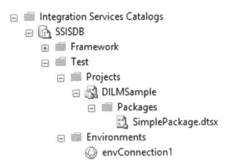

Figure 6-1. *The SSIS catalog as shown in the SSMS Object Explorer Integration Services Catalogs node*

Beneath the Integration Services Catalogs node we find the SSIS catalog named SSISDB. Two catalog folders are displayed, Framework and Test. The Test folder contains the Projects and Environments virtual folders. The Projects virtual folder contains the SSIS catalog project named DILMSample, which in turn contains the SSIS package named SimplePackage.dtsx. The Environments virtual folder contains the catalog environment named envConnection1.

You know, because you've done the work, that there's more there than meets the eye.

SSIS Catalog Environment Configuration

If you double-click envConnection1, you can see details of your catalog environment variable on the Variables page, shown in Figure 6-2.

Figure 6-2. *Viewing the Variables page of an SSIS catalog environment*

The Variables page contains details about SSIS catalog environment variables including name, data type, description, value, and whether the variable is sensitive.

SSIS Catalog Project Configuration

The Parameters tab on the Parameters page of the SSIS Catalog Project Configuration dialog lists SSIS project and package parameters, their container name, and value by default, as shown in Figure 6-3.

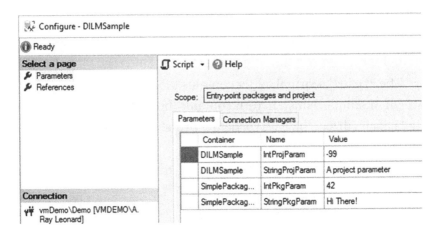

Figure 6-3. *Viewing project parameters and values for an SSIS catalog project*

The Connection Managers tab of the Parameters page contains a list of SSIS project and package connection managers and their properties, as shown in Figure 6-4.

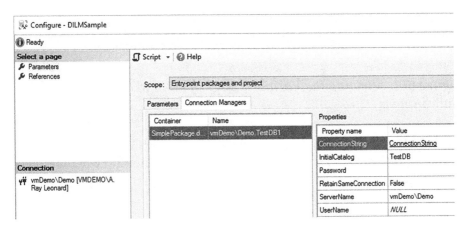

Figure 6-4. *Viewing connection manager parameters and values for an SSIS catalog project*

The References page of the SSIS Catalog Project Configure dialog contains a list of SSIS catalog environments the SSIS catalog project may reference at runtime, as shown in Figure 6-5.

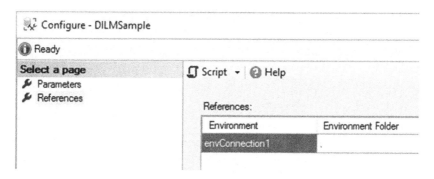

Figure 6-5. *Viewing project references for an SSIS catalog project*

That's a lot of right- and double-clicking just to see what's configured in an SSIS catalog project.

Catalog Browser

The SSIS catalog is filled with really cool and useful configuration information, but one has to know where to look and, in some cases, *where to look* isn't so obvious.

Enter Catalog Browser, a free utility that is part of the DILM Suite and available at `dilmsuite.com/catalog-browser`. Catalog Browser was built to surface the contents of the SSIS catalog in a single view: a tree that exposes all relevant SSIS catalog artifacts, properties, and configurations.

As shown in Figure 6-6, Catalog Browser surfaces the same metadata as the SSMS Object Explorer Integration Services Catalogs node.

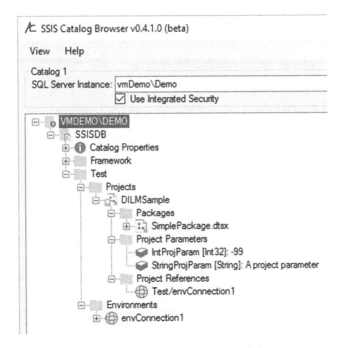

Figure 6-6. Catalog Browser surfacing part of the SSIS project and configurations metadata

Looking at Figure 6-6, though, you probably already see some differences between Catalog Browser and the SSMS Object Explorer Integration Services Catalogs node. Note the Project Parameters and Project References virtual folders present beneath the SSIS catalog project, in addition to the Packages virtual folder.

Expanding these virtual folders reveals the SSIS catalog project parameters and reference, as shown in Figure 6-7.

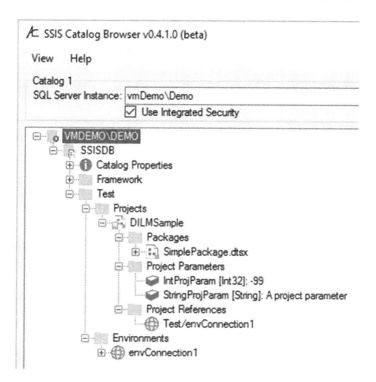

Figure 6-7. *SSIS catalog project parameters and references*

Remember in Figure 6-3 the SSMS Object Explorer Integration Services
Catalogs node surfaced *all* parameters: SSIS catalog project parameters
and SSIS package parameters. Where are the package parameters? They're
here in Catalog Browser. To view the package parameters, expand the
SimplePackage.dtsx SSIS package node, as shown in Figure 6-8.

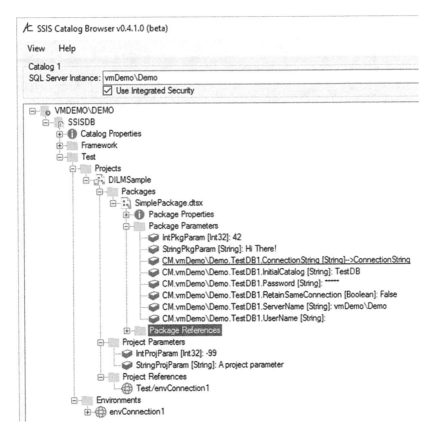

Figure 6-8. Viewing SSIS package parameters

Recall that connection manager properties are treated as parameters in the SSIS catalog. They are prefixed with "CM." You can see that the SSIS package connection manager vmDemo\Demo.TestDB1 connection string property is mapped to an SSIS catalog environment variable named ConnectionString.

To surface the reference used for the reference mapping, expand the Package References virtual folder, as shown in Figure 6-9.

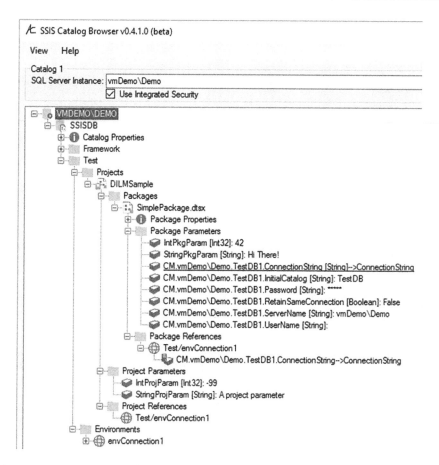

Figure 6-9. *Viewing the package reference*

Expanding the Package Reference virtual folder surfaces the Test/ envConection1 catalog environment. Expanding the Test/envConection1 catalog environment reveals that the catalog environment variable named ConnectionString is mapped to the vmDemo\Demo.TestDB1 connection string property.

But what's the value of the ConnectionString catalog environment variable? Expand the envConnection1 catalog environment in the Environments virtual folder to view the collection of catalog environment variables, their data types, and their values, as shown in Figure 6-10.

Figure 6-10. *Catalog environment variables, data types, and values*

SSIS package properties includes a Package Version property constructed from the Version Major, Version Minor, and Version Build properties of the SSIS package. Every time a developer saves an SSIS package, the Version Build property increments. It's possible to revise an SSIS package and "trick" the Version Build property by manually setting it. I have not yet found a valid use case for doing so to SSIS catalog-deployed SSIS packages.

The Package Version property can be used to detect different versions of SSIS packages deployed to an SSIS catalog. Because SSIS developers can manually set the Version Build property, Package Version is not a reliable indication.

The `Package Properties` virtual folder surfaces SSIS package metadata, as shown in Figure 6-11.

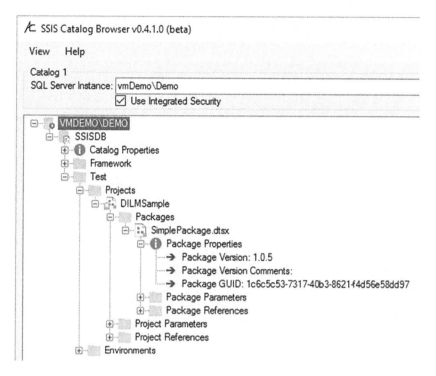

Figure 6-11. *SSIS package properties*

Catalog properties are handy for detecting differences in patch levels (via the Schema Build property). Catalog Version is a property exposed by Catalog Base, the custom catalog object that lies beneath Catalog Browser.

Catalog Base works with SSIS 2012, 2014, and 2016 catalogs.

The Catalog Properties virtual folder surfaces SSIS catalog metadata, as shown in Figure 6-12.

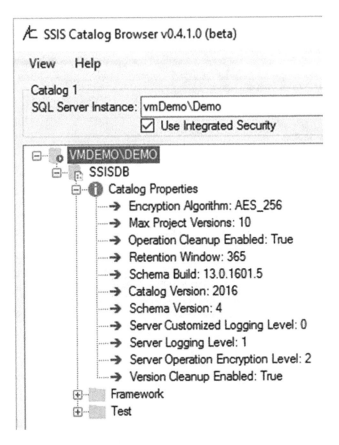

Figure 6-12. *SSIS catalog properties*

Conclusion

Catalog Browser surfaces SSIS catalog artifacts, configurations metadata, and artifact properties in a single view.

CHAPTER 7

SSIS Catalog Compare

Viewing the SSIS catalog contents, including SSIS catalog projects, packages, environments, environment variables, references, and reference mappings along with SSIS package and SSIS catalog properties, is helpful. But what if you want to see the differences between the contents of one SSIS catalog instance and another? Or, perhaps even more useful, how can you *know* the enterprise QA and Production SSIS catalog instances match?

Why I Built SSIS Catalog Compare, by Andy Leonard

My team built a fairly complex data integration solution for a client using SSIS. We tested the solution in two DevOps tiers, Test and UAT (User Acceptance Testing). We identified some issues and corrected them. It was then time to deploy to Production. My team and I were on standby during the Production deployment and initial Production tests.

Initially, everything failed.

We identified the root causes and corrected the issues, but we had egg on our collective faces with the business, and for good reason. We had assured them "we were doing it right." We were, with one exception. The

© Andy Leonard 2018
A. Leonard, *Data Integration Life Cycle Management with SSIS*,
https://doi.org/10.1007/978-1-4842-3276-7_7

enterprise data architect identified the gap with one very good question, "How can we *know* the Production and UAT SSIS catalogs are the same?" My response at the time, "[Pregnant pause while thinking... then] I don't know."

I built SSIS Catalog Compare so I—and my customers, and you—can answer that question.

SSIS Catalog Compare

You can begin by thinking of SSIS Catalog Compare as two Catalog Browsers. Like Catalog Browser, SSIS Catalog Compare uses Catalog Base, a custom catalog object. In SSIS Catalog Compare, Catalog Base is used to populate two trees, each representing a different SSIS catalog, as shown in Figure 7-1.

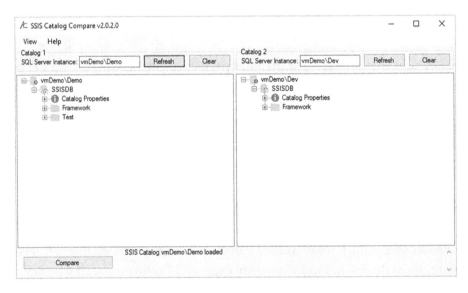

Figure 7-1. *SSIS Catalog Compare*

Once two catalogs are loaded, they may be compared by clicking the Compare button. As shown in Figure 7-2, SSIS Catalog Compare uses the italics font to indicate that a difference has been detected *beneath* a node and a different background color to indicate artifacts that are present in one SSIS catalog but missing from the other.

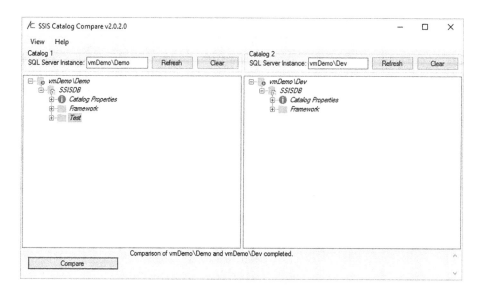

Figure 7-2. *After a Compare operation*

The Test catalog folder in the VmDemo\Demo catalog does not exist in the vmDemo\Dev catalog, hence the background color on the vmDemo\Demo\ SSISDB\Test node. The "deeper differences" indications (italics fonts) shown in Figure 7-2 indicate differences within the Framework catalog folders and between the catalog properties.

Expanding the Differences

One time-saver is Expand Differences, shown in Figure 7-3.

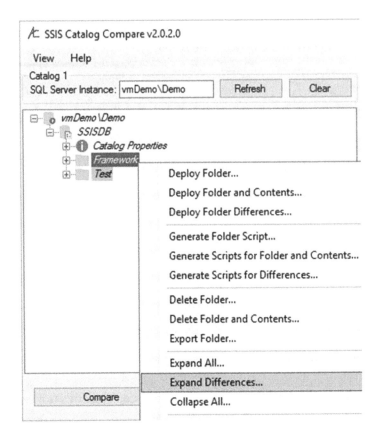

Figure 7-3. *Expand Differences*

Expand Differences will expand nodes *above* differences and the nodes that *are* different. In large SSIS catalog projects, catalog projects with lots of configurations metadata, or both, Expand Differences can reduce the number of nodes expanded. Expanding the differences in the Framework catalog folder for both catalogs, you see the Parent.dtsx SSIS package

SSISDB connection manager's ConnectionString property is configured for each server's local SQL Server instance, as shown in Figure 7-4.

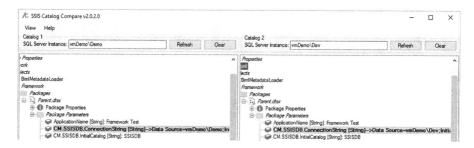

Figure 7-4. *Different ConnectionString property values*

This is a really good thing because, if these values matched, framework application executions in one catalog would start SSIS executions in another catalog. That could be bad.

Catalog Properties

I didn't discuss catalog properties in the section about Catalog Browser because I wanted to cover catalog properties here in more detail. If you collapse the Framework catalog folder and expand Catalog Properties, you see the difference is the Schema Build property, shown in Figure 7-5.

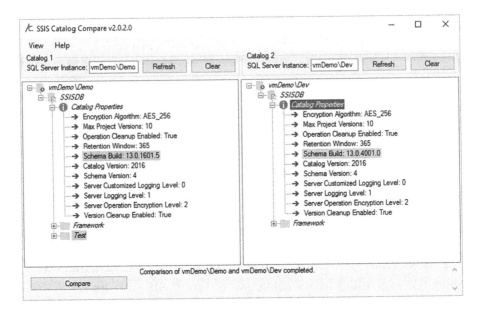

Figure 7-5. *Different values for the SSIS catalog Schema Build property*

Note from the property just beneath Schema Build that both of these SSIS catalogs are SSIS 2016. vmDemo\Demo's Schema Build version tells us that this catalog is the General Availability (or GA, formerly known as RTM [Release to Manufacturing]) version of SSIS 2016. vmDemo\Dev's catalog is an SSIS 2016 SP1 Schema Build version.

The Catalog Base object is built to allow SSIS Catalog Compare to compare SSIS catalogs from different releases and versions of SQL Server. For example, I could compare the contents of an SSIS 2012 catalog to those of an SSIS 2016 catalog. SSIS 2016 added a couple properties to the catalog properties, so you would see a couple properties marked on the 2016 side of the compare as missing from the 2012 side. But the Compare operation would succeed and produce accurate and useful results.

SSIS Catalog Compare Scripting

In many enterprises with two or more IT professionals, the professional who develops the software is not permitted to deploy that software. Large enterprises have entire teams dedicated to release management. Lifecycle management will help enterprises of any size reduce downtime and improve code supportability and maintainability. This holds for SSIS because data integration lifecycle management is just as vital as web, GUI, and middle-tier software lifecycle management.

SSIS Catalog Compare is designed to support DevOps and enterprise DILM.

You can script individual artifacts using SSIS Catalog Compare, but perhaps the more useful (and quicker) functionality is to script a catalog folder and all its contents, as shown in Figure 7-6.

Figure 7-6. *Preparing to generate scripts for a catalog folder and its contents*

When you click "Generate Scripts for Folder and Contents," SSIS Catalog Compare prompts you for a file system folder in which to store the scripts, as show in Figure 7-7.

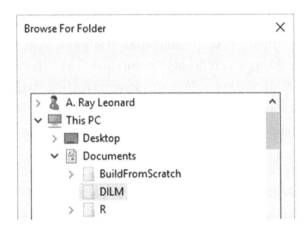

Figure 7-7. *Selecting a target file system folder for the scripts*

When you select a file system folder, SSIS Catalog Compare generates the scripts and ISPAC files to create the catalog folder and all its contents, as shown in Figure 7-8.

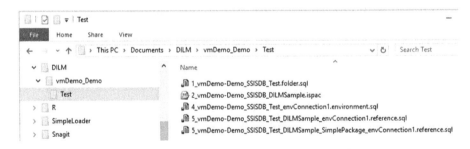

Figure 7-8. *Viewing the target file system folder for the scripts*

The scripts are numbered in an order that represents dependencies. For example, you cannot deploy an SSIS project using the ISPAC file, number 2, unless and until the SSIS catalog folder for that SSIS catalog project exists, script number 1.

Double-clicking the files in the order listed will create the Test catalog folder (script 1) on the target SSIS catalog, deploy the DILMSample SSIS project using the Integration Services Deployment Wizard GUI (you will need to select the Test catalog folder as the target catalog folder during deployment), create the envConnection1 catalog environment and its catalog environment variable(s), create a reference between the DILMSample SSIS project and envConnection1, and create *another* reference with reference mapping(s) between the SimplePackage.dtsx SSIS package and the envConnection1 catalog environment.

Why two reference files? Inside the SSIS catalog references for SSIS catalog projects and SSIS packages are distinct artifacts.

Creating a Catalog Folder

The scripts (and ISPAC) are idempotent, or re-executable, as shown in Figure 7-9.

```
1_vmDemo-Demo_SS...Ray Leonard (56))    ×
 1  /*
 2  Script Name: C:\Users\A. Ray Leonard\Documents\DILM\vmDemo_Demo\Test\\
 3  Generated From Catalog Instance: vmDemo\Demo
 4  Catalog Name: SSISDB
 5  Folder Name: Test
 6  Generated By: VMDEMO\A. Ray Leonard
 7  Generated Date: 8/8/2017 10:05:38 PM
 8  Generated From: CatalogBase v2.0.2.0 executing on: VMDEMO
 9  */
10
11  Use SSISDB
12  go
13
14  print 'Script Name: C:\Users\A. Ray Leonard\Documents\DILM\vmDemo_Demo
15  Generated From Catalog Instance: vmDemo\Demo
16  Catalog Name: SSISDB
17  Folder Name: Test
18  Generated By: VMDEMO\A. Ray Leonard
19  Generated Date: 8/8/2017 10:05:38 PM
20  Generated From: CatalogBase v2.0.2.0 executing on: VMDEMO'
```

Figure 7-9. *Idempotent Transact-SQL scripts*

If the Test catalog folder does not exist, the script creates it. If the Test catalog folder exists, the script outputs a message informing the executor of this fact.

The output messages are written to be copied and pasted into a ticket's Notes field before the ticket is closed. The messages provide detailed information about how and when the script was generated, by whom, when and where the script was executed, and by whom, as shown in Figure 7-10.

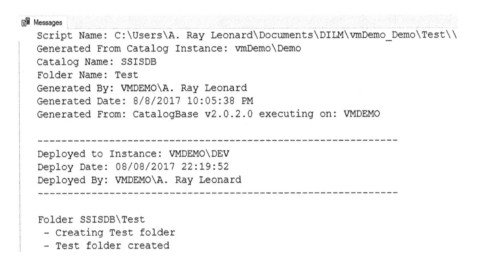

```
Messages
    Script Name: C:\Users\A. Ray Leonard\Documents\DILM\vmDemo_Demo\Test\\
    Generated From Catalog Instance: vmDemo\Demo
    Catalog Name: SSISDB
    Folder Name: Test
    Generated By: VMDEMO\A. Ray Leonard
    Generated Date: 8/8/2017 10:05:38 PM
    Generated From: CatalogBase v2.0.2.0 executing on: VMDEMO


    -----------------------------------------------------------
    Deployed to Instance: VMDEMO\DEV
    Deploy Date: 08/08/2017 22:19:52
    Deployed By: VMDEMO\A. Ray Leonard
    -----------------------------------------------------------

    Folder SSISDB\Test
     - Creating Test folder
     - Test folder created
```

Figure 7-10. Script output messages

Refreshing the SSIS catalog node in SSMS Object Explorer will reveal the Test catalog folder has been created, as show in Figure 7-11.

Figure 7-11. *Refreshing the SSIS catalog node*

Figure 7-12 shows the results of the refresh: the Test catalog folder has been created by the script.

Figure 7-12. *The Test catalog folder lives!*

I began this section stating, "The scripts (and ISPAC) are idempotent..." What happens if you re-execute the script you just used to create the Test catalog folder? Let's return to SSMS and try it. The results are shown in Figure 7-13.

```
Messages
    Script Name: C:\Users\A. Ray Leonard\Documents\DILM\vmDemo_Demo\Test\\
    Generated From Catalog Instance: vmDemo\Demo
    Catalog Name: SSISDB
    Folder Name: Test
    Generated By: VMDEMO\A. Ray Leonard
    Generated Date: 8/8/2017 10:05:38 PM
    Generated From: CatalogBase v2.0.2.0 executing on: VMDEMO

    ---------------------------------------------------------------
    Deployed to Instance: VMDEMO\DEV
    Deploy Date: 08/09/2017 06:27:00
    Deployed By: VMDEMO\A. Ray Leonard
    ---------------------------------------------------------------

    Folder SSISDB\Test
     - Test folder already exists.
     - Setting Test folder description to ""
     - Test folder description set to ""
```

Figure 7-13. *Re-executing the Catalog Folder script*

Please note the message returned: "Test folder already exists." The Test catalog folder was not harmed by re-executing the script. The script simply checks for the existence of the catalog folder and creates it if it does not exist. If the catalog folder exists, the script returns a message. The Transact-SQL that performs this operation is shown in Figure 7-14.

```
print 'Folder SSISDB\Test'
If Not Exists(Select *
                From SSISDB.[catalog].folders
                Where name = N'Test')
  begin
   print ' - Creating Test folder'
   declare @folder_id bigint
   Exec SSISDB.[catalog].create_folder
        @folder_name = N'Test'
      , @folder_id = @folder_id OUTPUT
   print ' - Test folder created'
  end
 else
  begin
   print ' - Test folder already exists.'
  end
```

Figure 7-14. *Transact-SQL that first checks for catalog folder existence*

If you refresh SSIS catalog Compare Catalog 2, you now see the Test catalog folder, as shown in Figure 7-15.

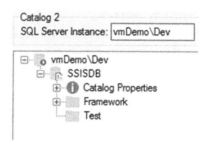

Figure 7-15. *The Test catalog folder created*

Deploying the SSIS Project

To deploy the SSIS project, double-click (or right-click and click Open) the ISPAC file, as shown in Figure 7-16.

Figure 7-16. Opening the ISPAC file

The Integration Services Deployment Wizard starts; this is the same wizard used to deploy SSIS projects from SQL Server Data Tools (SSDT). Stepping through the wizard, the first stop is the Select Source page shown in Figure 7-17.

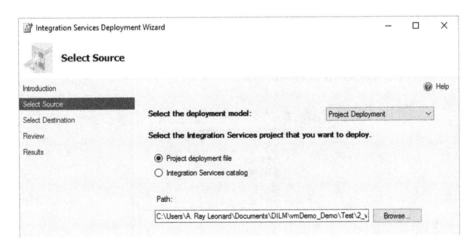

Figure 7-17. The Integration Services Deployment Wizard Select Source page

This page surfaces a lot of functionality. The Deployment Model dropdown is used to select project or package deployment. Beginning with SSIS 2016, operators have the option of deploying the entire SSIS project, which was the only option available in SSIS 2012 and 2014, or deploying a single SSIS package. Operators may also select the type of SSIS project source. There are two options available: a project deployment file or an Integration Services catalog. Since you started this exercise by opening an ISPAC file, the project deployment file option is selected for you.

If you select the Integration Services catalog option, the Select Source page presents catalog project settings that may be configured for an SSIS catalog project deployed to a different SSIS catalog, as shown in Figure 7-18.

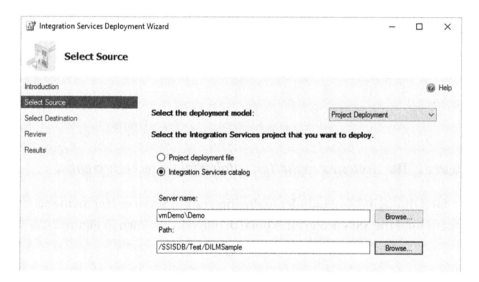

Figure 7-18. *Deploying from one SSIS catalog to another*

The remainder of the Integration Services Deployment Wizard pages and process are the same as those covered in Chapter 4. On the Select Destination page, enter the name of the SQL Server instance that hosts the target SSIS catalog. You can then browse to the newly-created catalog folder, shown in Figure 7-19.

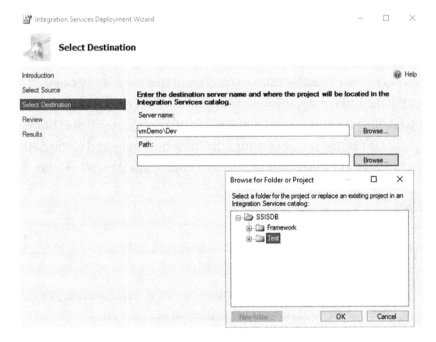

Figure 7-19. Browsing to the Test catalog folder recently created

Step through the remainder of the Integration Services Deployment Wizard until the SSIS project has been deployed, as shown in Figure 7-20.

Figure 7-20. *A successful deployment*

Refresh SSIS Catalog Compare to see that the SSIS catalog project now exists, as shown in Figure 7-21.

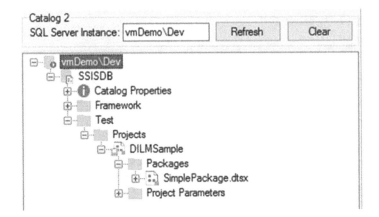

Figure 7-21. *Viewing the DILMSample SSIS catalog project*

As with the Catalog Folder script, ISPAC files are re-executable. When an ISPAC file is re-executed, a new version of the SSIS project is deployed to the target SSIS catalog.

Deploying the Literal Overrides and Catalog Environment

SSIS catalog literal overrides and environment scripts are similar because both contain values, either literal override values or values for catalog environment variables. Value parameters reside at the top of the Transact-SQL script generated and may be modified by the operator prior to deployment to the target SSIS catalog, as shown in Figure 7-22.

```
 1 ⊟ -- envConnection1 ENVIRONMENT VARIABLE VALUES --
 2
 3   | -- Environment Variable Test\envConnection1\ConnectionString
 4 ⊟Declare @ConnectionString_0 sql_variant = N'Data Source=vmDemo\Dev;Initial Catalog=TestDB;
 5
 6 ⊟ --------------------------------
 7
 8   |/*
 9   |Script Name: C:\Users\A. Ray Leonard\Documents\DILM\vmDemo_Demo\Test\\4_vmDemo-Demo_SSISDB
10   |Generated From Catalog Instance: vmDemo\Demo
11   |Catalog Name: SSISDB
12   |Folder Name: Test
13   |Environment Name: envConnection1
14   |Generated By: VMDEMO\A. Ray Leonard
15   |Generated Date: 8/8/2017 10:05:38 PM
16   |Generated From: CatalogBase v2.0.2.0 executing on: VMDEMO
17   |*/
18
19 ⊟print 'Script Name: C:\Users\A. Ray Leonard\Documents\DILM\vmDemo_Demo\Test\\4_vmDemo-Demo
20   |Generated From Catalog Instance: vmDemo\Demo
21   |Catalog Name: SSISDB
```

Figure 7-22. *Editing an SSIS catalog environment script prior to execution*

As with the SSIS Catalog Folder script, the Catalog Environment script provides rich feedback messages, as shown in Figure 7-23.

```
Script Name: C:\Users\A. Ray Leonard\Documents\DILM\vmDemo_Demo\
Generated From Catalog Instance: vmDemo\Demo
Catalog Name: SSISDB
Folder Name: Test
Environment Name: envConnection1
Generated By: VMDEMO\A. Ray Leonard
Generated Date: 8/8/2017 10:05:38 PM
Generated From: CatalogBase v2.0.2.0 executing on: VMDEMO


-----------------------------------------------------------
Deployed to Instance: VMDEMO\DEV
Deploy Date: 08/09/2017 07:04:43
Deployed By: VMDEMO\A. Ray Leonard
-----------------------------------------------------------

Check for folder: Test
 - Test folder exists.

Environment SSISDB\Test\envConnection1
```

Figure 7-23. *Messages from the Catalog Environment Script execution*

Please note the Catalog Environment script first checks for the existence on the target catalog folder and provides feedback in message on its existence. If the target folder does not exist, the Catalog Environment script will fail. Catalog environment variables are created in the Catalog Environment script.

Deploying Project and Package References

Project Reference scripts check for the existence of the catalog folder, catalog project, and catalog environment, as shown in Figure 7-24.

```
print 'Check for folder: Test '
If Not Exists(Select name
                From SSISDB.[catalog].folders
                Where name = N'Test')
  begin
    set @ErrMsg = ' - Test does not exist.'
    raisError(@ErrMsg, 16, 1)
    return
  end
Else
  begin
    print ' - Test folder exists.'
  end
print ''

print 'Check for project: DILMSample '
If Not Exists(Select name
                From SSISDB.[catalog].projects
                Where name = N'DILMSample')
  begin
    set @ErrMsg = ' - DILMSample project does not exist.'
    raisError(@ErrMsg, 16, 1)
    return
  end
Else
  begin
    print ' - DILMSample project exists.'
  end
print ''

print 'Check for environment: envConnection1 '
If Not Exists(Select name
                From SSISDB.[catalog].environments
                Where name = N'envConnection1')
  begin
    set @ErrMsg = ' - envConnection1 environment does not exist.'
    raisError(@ErrMsg, 16, 1)
    return
  end
```

Figure 7-24. *The Project Reference script checks for catalog folder, project, and environment*

When executed for the first time, the Project Reference script returns messages similar to those shown in Figure 7-25.

```
Messages
    Script Name: C:\Users\A. Ray Leonard\Documents\DILM\vmDemo_Demo\TestG
    Catalog Name: SSISDB
    Folder Name: Test
    Project Name: DILMSample
    Reference Name: Test/envConnection1
    Environment Name: envConnection1
    Generated By: VMDEMO\A. Ray Leonard
    Generated Date: 8/8/2017 10:05:38 PM
    Generated From: CatalogBase v2.0.2.0 executing on: VMDEMO

    ----------------------------------------------------------------
    Deployed to Instance: VMDEMO\DEV
    Deploy Date: 08/09/2017 19:46:38
    Deployed By: VMDEMO\A. Ray Leonard
    ----------------------------------------------------------------

    Check for folder: Test
     - Test folder exists.

    Check for project: DILMSample
     - DILMSample project exists.

    Check for environment: envConnection1
     - envConnection1 environment exists.

    Reference SSISDB\Test\DILMSample\[.|Test/envConnection1]
      - Creating Reference SSISDB\Test\DILMSample\[.|Test/envConnection1]
      - Reference SSISDB\Test\DILMSample\[.|Test/envConnection1] created
```

Figure 7-25. *Project Reference script feedback*

If the Project Reference script is re-executed, the messages reveal that the project reference already exists, as shown in Figure 7-26.

```
Messages
Script Name: C:\Users\A. Ray Leonard\Documents\DILM\vmDemo_Demo\TestGenerate
Catalog Name: SSISDB
Folder Name: Test
Project Name: DILMSample
Reference Name: Test/envConnection1
Environment Name: envConnection1
Generated By: VMDEMO\A. Ray Leonard
Generated Date: 8/8/2017 10:05:38 PM
Generated From: CatalogBase v2.0.2.0 executing on: VMDEMO

-----------------------------------------------------------
Deployed to Instance: VMDEMO\DEV
Deploy Date: 08/09/2017 19:47:00
Deployed By: VMDEMO\A. Ray Leonard
-----------------------------------------------------------

Check for folder: Test
 - Test folder exists.

Check for project: DILMSample
 - DILMSample project exists.

Check for environment: envConnection1
 - envConnection1 environment exists.

Reference SSISDB\Test\DILMSample\[.|Test/envConnection1]
 - Reference SSISDB\Test\DILMSample\[.|Test/envConnection1] already exists.
```

Figure 7-26. *Re-executing the Project Reference script*

The Package Reference script is most complex among the scripts generated by SSIS Catalog Compare. As shown in Figure 7-27, the Package Reference script includes checks for catalog folder, project, environment, and reference.

```
 91 ⊟ begin
 92   print ' - Creating Reference SSISDB\Test\DILMSample\DILMSample\[.|Test/envConnection1]'
 93   Declare @reference_id bigint
 94 ⊟ Exec [SSISDB].[catalog].[create_environment_reference]
 95       @environment_name = N'envConnection1'
 96     , @reference_id = @reference_id OUTPUT
 97     , @project_name = N'DILMSample'
 98     , @folder_name = N'Test'
 99     , @environment_folder_name = NULL
100     , @reference_type = R
101   print ' - Reference SSISDB\Test\DILMSample\DILMSample\[.|Test/envConnection1] created'
102   end
103 else print ' - Reference SSISDB\Test\DILMSample\DILMSample\[.|Test/envConnection1] already exists.'
104
105
106 print ''
107   -- Reference Project Parameter Mapping CM.vmDemo\Demo.TestDB1.ConnectionString-->ConnectionString
108 print ' - Reference Project Parameter Mapping CM.vmDemo\Demo.TestDB1.ConnectionString-->ConnectionString'
109 print ' - Clear Reference Package or Project Parameter Mapping CM.vmDemo\Demo.TestDB1.ConnectionString-->ConnectionString'
110 ⊟Exec [SSISDB].[catalog].[clear_object_parameter_value]
111       @object_type = 30 -- package
112     , @object_name = N'SimplePackage.dtsx'
113     , @parameter_name = N'CM.vmDemo\Demo.TestDB1.ConnectionString'
114     , @folder_name = N'Test'
115     , @project_name = N'DILMSample'
116
117 print ' - Reference Project Parameter Mapping CM.vmDemo\Demo.TestDB1.ConnectionString-->ConnectionString cleared'
118 print ''
119 print ' - Add or Update Reference Package or Project Parameter Mapping CM.vmDemo\Demo.TestDB1.ConnectionString-->ConnectionString'
120 ⊟Exec [SSISDB].[catalog].[set_object_parameter_value]
121       @object_type = 30 -- package
122     , @parameter_name = N'CM.vmDemo\Demo.TestDB1.ConnectionString'
123     , @object_name = N'SimplePackage.dtsx'
124     , @folder_name = N'Test'
125     , @project_name = N'DILMSample'
126     , @parameter_value = N'ConnectionString'
127     , @value_type = 'R'
128
129 print ' - Reference Project Parameter Mapping CM.vmDemo\Demo.TestDB1.ConnectionString-->ConnectionString added / updated'
130 print ''
```

Figure 7-27. *Existence checks in the Package Reference script*

The Package Reference script always clears the existing value in the reference mapping before setting it.

As one might imagine, there are several messages returned from execution of the Package Reference script and they are shown in Figure 7-28.

Figure 7-28. *Message returned from Package Reference script execution*

Testing with SSIS Catalog Compare

Return to SSIS Catalog Compare and right-click the Compare button to "Refresh Both TreeViews and Compare," as shown in Figure 7-29.

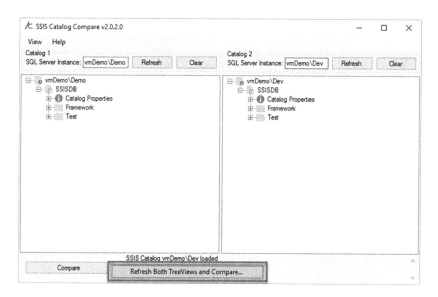

Figure 7-29. *Refreshing both TreeViews and comparing*

What's this? Didn't I just walk through deploying all these scripted artifacts to the target SSIS catalog? Why doesn't Figure 7-30 show everything matching? Please remember you updated the value of the ConnectionString catalog environment variable before you executed the Catalog Environment script. Figure 7-30 shows the difference that exists between the Test catalog folders in the SSIS catalog instances.

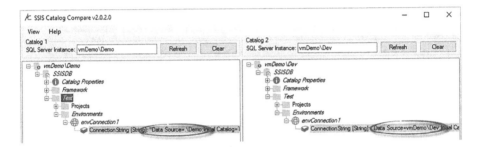

Figure 7-30. *Different data source values*

Now what? These values are, after all, *supposed* to be different. It's *bad* if they're the same, in fact. Fear not. Click View ➤ Options, as shown in Figure 7-31.

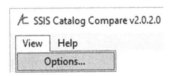

Figure 7-31. *Opening SSIS Catalog Compare options*

You can ignore catalog environment variable values by checking the checkbox shown in Figure 7-32.

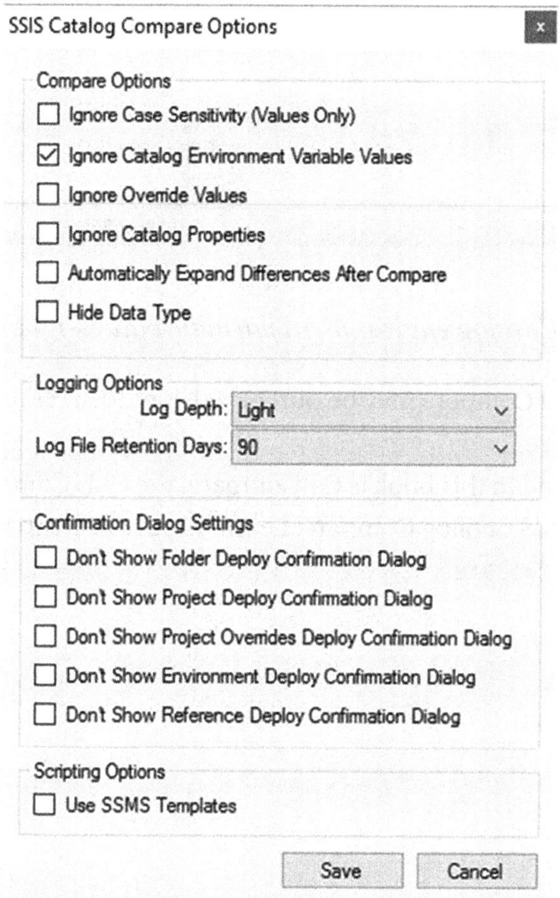

Figure 7-32. *SSIS Catalog Compare options*

Once catalog environment variable values are ignored, a re-compare operation shows that the Test catalog folders in your catalogs match. Expanding the envConnection1 catalog environment to view the values of the ConnectionString catalog environment variable shows the values have not changed; they're still different, and merely ignored, as shown in Figure 7-33.

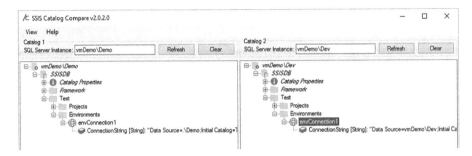

Figure 7-33. *Catalog environment variable values, ignored*

SSIS Catalog Compare may be purchased at `dilmsuite.com/ssis-catalog-compare`.

Not discussed in this book is CatCompare, the CLI (Command-Line Interface) for SSIS Catalog Compare. Learn more at `dilmsuite.com/ssis-catalog-compare`.

CHAPTER 8

SSIS Framework Community Edition

A best practice in SSIS development is to build small, unit-of-work SSIS packages. There are several reasons for this:

- **Decoupling**: SSIS is software development and a best practice with software development is separation of concerns. Separation of concerns is primarily achieved by decoupling. One way to decouple SSIS is to build small, single-function SSIS packages.

- **Testing**: If an SSIS package contains seven data flow tasks and the design of a source table changes and breaks one data flow task, all tasks in the SSIS package should be tested. Fewer data flow tasks means less and quicker testing.

- **Support**: If all SSIS packages contain the minimum number of data flow tasks (optimally one) and a package execution fails in the middle of the night, on-call support has a pretty good idea where to begin troubleshooting.

© Andy Leonard 2018
A. Leonard, *Data Integration Life Cycle Management with SSIS*,
https://doi.org/10.1007/978-1-4842-3276-7_8

While these are good and valid reasons to build SSIS solutions with several smaller SSIS packages, following this advice causes other issues. One issue is you now have a bunch of SSIS packages that require executing in some order. What's a data integration developer to do?

SSIS Framework Community Edition

Consider the SSIS Framework Community Edition, a free and open-source solution available at dilmsuite.com/ssis-framework-community-edition. SSIS Framework Community Edition allows the execution of one or more SSIS packages in a specified execution order by executing a single stored procedure and passing it a single argument. For example, I can execute a test framework application with the following Transact-SQL statement:

```
exec custom.execute_catalog_parent_package @application_name =
'Framework Test '
```

Continuing my theme of "there's no free lunch," SSIS execution frameworks greatly simplify execution commands like the one listed above but they create another issue: the need to manage a lot of metadata. SSIS Framework Community Edition relies on metadata to build a *framework application*, mentioned earlier. A framework application is a collection of SSIS packages configured to execute in a specified order. If you build idempotent (re-executable) Transact-SQL that includes print statements (to inform you of what the T-SQL is doing) and use any kind of formatting, you're looking at 30-40 lines of Transact-SQL per SSIS package. That's a lot of T-SQL.

Help for SSIS Catalog Projects Already Deployed

Perhaps you are reading this and thinking, "That's awesome, but I have a bajillion SSIS packages already deployed to my SSIS catalog. What about them?" I wrote a blog post called "Adding an SSIS Application to SSIS Framework Community Edition" at andyleonard.blog/2017/07/26/ adding-an-ssis-application-to-ssis-framework-community-edition. I included a script at the end of that post that uses three parameters (Framework Application Name, Catalog Folder Name, and Catalog Project Name) and from those three pieces of metadata loads the metadata for a new framework application into SSIS Framework Community Edition's metadata tables, as shown in Figure 8-1.

```
1    Use SSISDB
2    go
3
4   declare @frameworkApplicationName varchar(255) = N'Load AdventureWorks2014 Stage'
5    declare @catalogFolderName nvarchar(128) = N'Stage'
6    declare @catalogProjectName nvarchar(128) = N'AdventureWorks2014_Stage_Loader'
7    declare @packageName nvarchar(260)
8    declare @sql nvarchar(4000)
9    declare @CrLf char(2) = Char(13) + Char(10)
10   declare @ApplicationID int
11   declare @PackageID int
12   declare @ExecutionOrder int = 10
13   declare @ExecFlag bit = 1
14
15  declare curPackages Cursor For
16  Select p.[name] As PackageName
17   From [catalog].packages p
18   Join [catalog].projects pr
19   On pr.project_id = p.project_id
20   Join [catalog].folders f
21   On f.folder_id = pr.folder_id
22   Where pr.[name] = @catalogProjectName
23   And f.[name] = @catalogFolderName
```

Figure 8-1. *Building a framework application from an SSIS catalog project*

The script reads the SSIS catalog project metadata shown in Figure 8-2 and loads the framework application metadata into SSIS Framework Community Edition metadata tables in a few seconds.

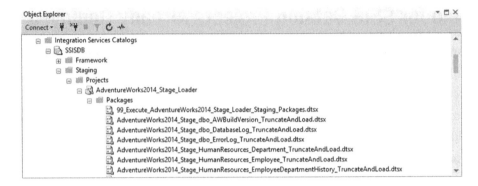

Figure 8-2. *The SSIS catalog project*

The framework application named "Load AdventureWorks2014 Stage" that contains 71 SSIS packages can now be executed with the following Transact-SQL statement:

```
exec custom.execute_catalog_parent_package @application_name =
'Load AdventureWorks2014 Stage'
```

Viewing SSIS Catalog Reports

You can view the executions of these 71 SSIS packages using the Catalog Reporting solution built into SSMS. To view all SSIS package executions, right-click the SSMS Object Explorer Integration Services Catalogs node's SSISDB node, hover over Reports, hover over Standard Reports, and click All Executions, as shown in Figure 8-3.

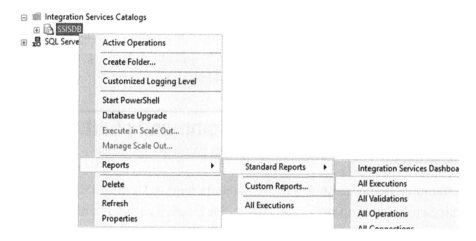

Figure 8-3. *Opening the built-in SSIS catalog reports*

The All Executions report displays and surfaces SSIS package execution logs, as shown in Figure 8-4.

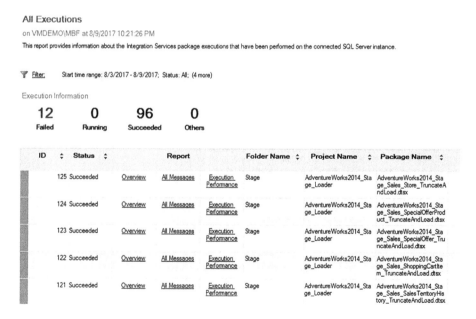

Figure 8-4. *The All Executions report*

To summarize, you supplied three pieces of metadata to a Transact-SQL script that built a framework application containing 71 SSIS packages, and then executed those 71 SSIS packages by starting a single stored procedure and passing it one parameter value.

Viewing SSIS Framework Community Edition Metadata

As mentioned, there's quite a bit of metadata required for the SSIS Framework Community Edition. The script we used earlier is a nice piece of automation for entering SSIS Framework Community Edition metadata, but what happens when we want to *view* the framework applications already stored?

Enter Framework Browser, another free utility from DILM Suite that you can download at dilmsuite.com/framework-browser, shown in Figure 8-5.

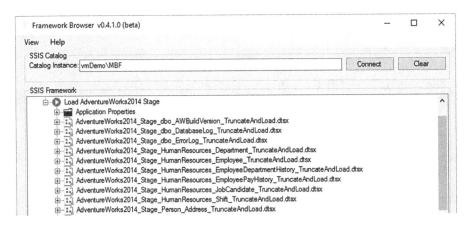

Figure 8-5. *The framework application's Load AdventureWorks2014 stage*

A framework application is a collection of SSIS packages, called *application packages* in the framework, that execute in a specified order. Framework Browser lists application packages in the order they execute.

If you expand the `Application Properties` virtual folder, you see framework application metadata. Expand the Application Package node and the Application Package Properties node to surface application package metadata, as shown in Figure 8-6.

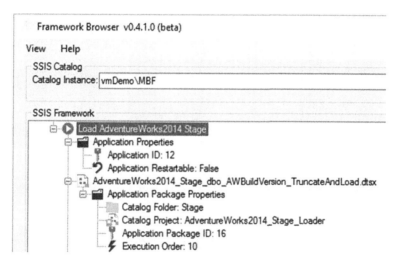

Figure 8-6. *Surfacing application and application package framework metadata*

Framework Browser is another free utility from DILM Suite.

CHAPTER 9

Catalog Reports

You've looked at the SSMS Catalog Reports solution built into SQL Server Management Studio (SSMS) a few times in your journey thus far, most recently in the previous chapter. As a data integration architect, I find these reports awesome, with a couple caveats:

1. I cannot select text for copy and paste.

2. In order to view SSMS Catalog Reports, one must install SSMS.

Regarding the second point, there are people in the enterprise who have a legitimate need to view the execution of data integration processes in the enterprise Production environment, but have no business having the remainder of SSMS installed on their machine, much less with access to the enterprise Production environment. SSMS is a fantastic utility for managing data and administering all aspects of SQL Server. To install SSMS for the sole purpose of granting someone access to the SSMS Catalog Reports is overkill.

Please take a look at Catalog Reports, a free and open-source solution that's part of the DILM Suite, at `dilmsuite.com/catalog-reports`.

Catalog Reports are designed to look and feel similar to the SSMS version, but they reside in SQL Server Reporting Services (SSRS). Look at the Executions Report shown in Figure 9-1.

© Andy Leonard 2018
A. Leonard, *Data Integration Life Cycle Management with SSIS*,
https://doi.org/10.1007/978-1-4842-3276-7_9

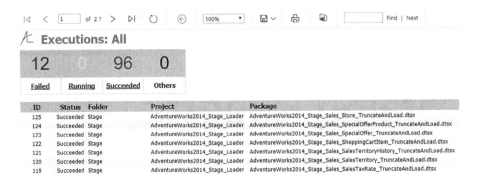

Figure 9-1. DILM Suite Catalog Reports Executions Report

DILM Suite Catalog Reports surface the same logs and data shown in the SSMS Catalog Reports without requiring the installation of SSMS. Because the solution is open source, SSRS developers can edit the reports to add corporate logos, apply enterprise color schemes, or include additional data.

Report viewers can select and copy text from their browser displaying the reports. There are options for exporting the contents of the report, as shown in Figure 9-2.

Figure 9-2. *Report export options*

The right side of the Executions Report contains links to other reports in the solution: Overview, Messages, and Performance (shown in Figure 9-3).

Package	Duration	Other Reports			Start Time
AdventureWorks2014_Stage_Sales_Store_TruncateAndLoad.dtsx	1.707	Overview	Messages	Performance	8/9/2017 10:19:19 PM
AdventureWorks2014_Stage_Sales_SpecialOfferProduct_TruncateAndLoad.dtsx	1.635	Overview	Messages	Performance	8/9/2017 10:19:17 PM
AdventureWorks2014_Stage_Sales_SpecialOffer_TruncateAndLoad.dtsx	1.645	Overview	Messages	Performance	8/9/2017 10:19:14 PM
AdventureWorks2014_Stage_Sales_ShoppingCartItem_TruncateAndLoad.dtsx	1.692	Overview	Messages	Performance	8/9/2017 10:19:11 PM
AdventureWorks2014_Stage_Sales_SalesTerritoryHistory_TruncateAndLoad.dtsx	1.625	Overview	Messages	Performance	8/9/2017 10:19:07 PM
AdventureWorks2014_Stage_Sales_SalesTerritory_TruncateAndLoad.dtsx	1.627	Overview	Messages	Performance	8/9/2017 10:19:04 PM
AdventureWorks2014_Stage_Sales_SalesTaxRate_TruncateAndLoad.dtsx	1.254	Overview	Messages	Performance	8/9/2017 10:19:00 PM
AdventureWorks2014_Stage_Sales_SalesReason_TruncateAndLoad.dtsx	1.222	Overview	Messages	Performance	8/9/2017 10:18:58 PM
AdventureWorks2014_Stage_Sales_SalesPersonQuotaHistory_TruncateAndLoad.dtsx	1.221	Overview	Messages	Performance	8/9/2017 10:18:54 PM

Figure 9-3. *More fields in the Executions Report*

Click the Overview link for the top-most SSIS package execution to open the Overview Report. The Overview Report surfaces a summary of SSIS package execution grouped by execution path (individual executables in the SSIS package) in the table on the left side of the report. This table is useful for determining the longest-running part of your SSIS package.

The Execution Information table displays operational log data such as SSIS package execution status, duration, start time, and the name of the catalog environment referenced for this execution. The Execution Parameters table displays SSIS catalog execution parameter settings and any parameters overridden or referenced for this execution, as shown in Figure 9-4.

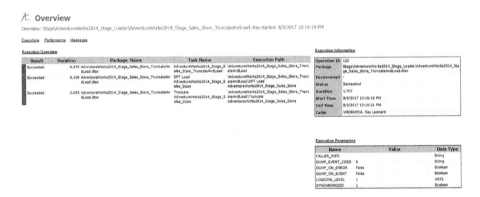

Figure 9-4. *DILM Suite Catalog Reports Overview Report*

The DILM Suite Overview Report includes navigation links at the top of the report to facilitate navigation to the Executions, Performance, and Messages reports. Click the Messages link to view the Messages Report, as shown in Figure 9-5.

Messages

Messages: Stage\AdventureWorks2014_Stage_Loader\AdventureWorks2014_Stage_Sales_Store_TruncateAndLoad.dtsx started: 8/9/2017

Executions Overview Performance

Event	Time	Message	Source
OnPostExecute	8/9/2017 10:19:21 PM	AdventureWorks2014_Stage_Sales_Store_TruncateAndLoad:Finished, 10:19:21 PM, Elapsed time: 00:00:00.375.	AdventureWorks2014_Stage_Sales_Store_TruncateAndLoad
OnPostExecute	8/9/2017 10:19:21 PM	DFT Load AdventureWorks2014_Stage_Sales_Store:Finished, 10:19:21 PM, Elapsed time: 00:00:00.109.	DFT Load AdventureWorks2014_Stage_Sales_Store
OnInformation	8/9/2017 10:19:21 PM	DFT Load AdventureWorks2014_Stage_Sales_Store:Information: Post Execute phase is beginning.	DFT Load AdventureWorks2014_Stage_Sales_Store
OnInformation	8/9/2017 10:19:21 PM	DFT Load AdventureWorks2014_Stage_Sales_Store:Information: "Write AdventureWorks2014_Stage_Sales_Store" wrote 701 rows.	DFT Load AdventureWorks2014_Stage_Sales_Store

Figure 9-5. *DILM Suite Catalog Reports Messages Report*

The Messages report lists every message logged by the execution of the SSIS package, when it was logged, the event that raised the message, and the name of the executable that raised the event.

The Performance report displays a graph of execution durations for previous successful executions, as shown in Figure 9-6.

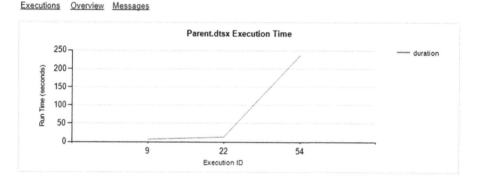

Figure 9-6. *DILM Suite Catalog Reports Performance Report*

The DILM Suite Catalog Reports solution is free and open-source, and addresses a couple issues with SSMS Catalog Reports.

CHAPTER 10

BimlExpress Metadata Framework

Business Intelligence Markup Language (Biml) is an XML-based language that increases data integration developer productivity and improves SSIS code quality. BimlExpress is free and integrates into SQL Server Data Tools (SSDT). The BimlExpress Metadata Framework is designed to encourage thinking about the possibilities when one combines the power of Biml with metadata.

You can learn more about Biml at varigence.com/biml and at bimlscript.com. You can obtain BimlExpress at `varigence.com/bimlexpress`. You can obtain a copy of the BimlExpress Metadata Framework project at `dilmsuite.com/biml-express-metadata-framework`.

When BimlExpress is installed, a developer can access the BimlExpress menu in SSDT. The first document a developer should open is the README file, shown in Figure 10-1.

© Andy Leonard 2018
A. Leonard, *Data Integration Life Cycle Management with SSIS*,
https://doi.org/10.1007/978-1-4842-3276-7_10

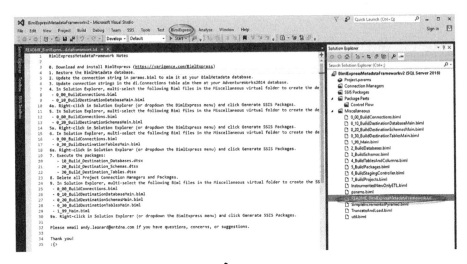

Figure 10-1. *Viewing the BimlExpress Metadata Framework project in SSDT*

The instructions in the README file walk a developer through the steps required to use the BimlExpress Metadata Framework. I will follow most of those steps in this chapter. You should follow them, too, if you desire to use the BimlExpress Metadata Framework.

Downloading and Installing BimlExpress

The first step is to download BimlExpress from varigence.com, as shown in Figure 10-2.

Figure 10-2. *Downloading BimlExpress*

When the download is complete, execute the `.vsix` file to install BimlExpress, as shown in Figure 10-3.

Figure 10-3. *Installing BimlExpress*

Accept the License Agreement, as shown in Figure 10-4.

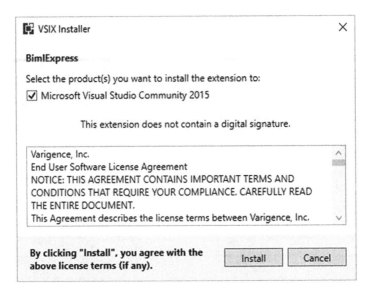

Figure 10-4. *Accepting the License Agreement*

Click the Install button to install BimlExpress.

When the installation completes, the VSIX Installer will display a notification similar to that shown in Figure 10-5.

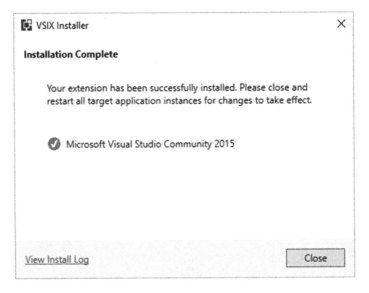

Figure 10-5. *BimlExpress installation is complete*

Click the Close button and open SQL Server Data Tools (SSDT).
Click Tools ➤ Extensions and Updates, as shown in Figure 10-6.

Figure 10-6.   *Opening Extensions and Updates*

The Extensions and Updates dialog is where you manage BimlExpress
and other SSDT plugins, as shown in Figure 10-7.

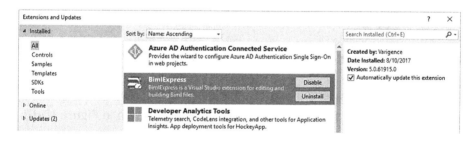

Figure 10-7.   *The Extensions and Updates dialog*

If you see the BimlExpress menu item shown in Figure 10-8,
BimlExpress is installed and enabled.

Figure 10-8. *BimlExpress installed and enabled*

Downloading BimlExpress Metadata Framework

Let's next download the BimlExpress Metadata Framework code from
dilmsuite.com/biml-express-metadata-framework, as shown in
Figure 10-9.

Figure 10-9. *Downloading BimlExpress Metadata Framework*

The BimlExpress Metadata Framework file is a text file named
BimlExpressMetadataFramewor.renametozip.txt, shown in Figure 10-10.

Name

Biml Express Metadata Framework

BimlExpressMetadataFramework.renametozip

Figure 10-10. *The BimlExpress Metadata Framework file*

One the file is downloaded, rename it as shown in Figure 10-11.

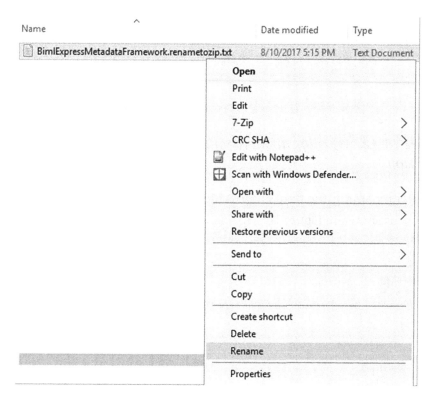

Figure 10-11. *Preparing to rename the Biml Express Metadata Framework Download file*

Changing the file extension to "zip" will trigger the warning shown in Figure 10-12.

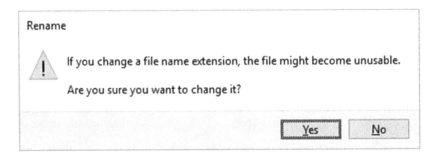

Figure 10-12. *Warning about renaming a file and changing the extension*

After renaming, the Biml Express Metadata Framework Download file appears as shown in Figure 10-13.

Figure 10-13. *The renamed Biml Express Metadata Framework Download file*

Right-click the Biml Express Metadata Framework file and click Extract All, as shown in Figure 10-14.

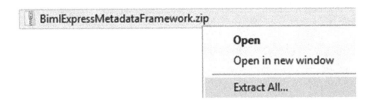

Figure 10-14. *Preparing to extract the Biml Express Metadata Framework file*

The Extract Compressed (Zipped) Folders dialog displays as shown in Figure 10-15.

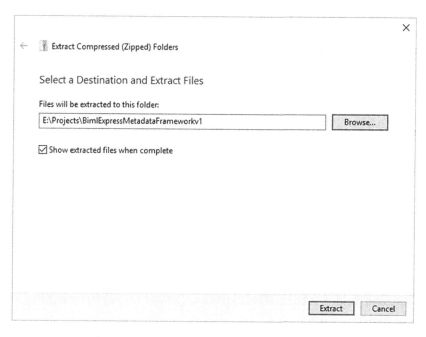

Figure 10-15. *Choosing a folder for the extracted files*

Click the Extract button to extract the compressed files.

After the contents of the zip file have been extracted, browse to the folder and open the BimlExpressMetadataFramework.sln file, as shown in Figure 10-16.

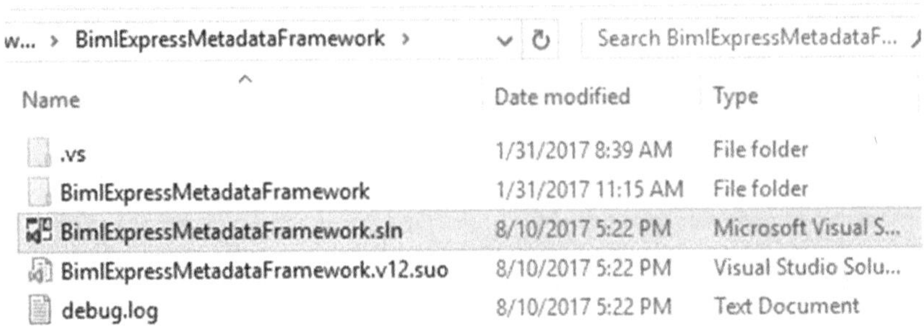

Figure 10-16. *Opening the BimlExpressMetadataFramework.sln file*

Following the README File Instructions

At the time of this writing, the README file included with the BimlExpressMetadataFramework project reads as follows:

```
BimlExpressMetadataFramework Notes

0. Download and install BimlExpress (https://varigence.com/
BimlExpress)
1. Restore the BimlMetadata database.
2. Update the connection string in params.biml to aim it at
your BimlMetadata database.
3. Update connection strings in the di.Connections table aim
them at your AdventureWorks2014 database.
4. In Solution Explorer, multi-select the following Biml files
in the Miscellaneous virtual folder to create the destination
Database:
 - 0_00_BuildConnections.biml
 - 0_10_BuildDestinationDatabaseMain.biml
4a. Right-click in Solution Explorer (or dropdown the
BimlExpress menu) and click Generate SSIS Packages.
```

5. In Solution Explorer, multi-select the following Biml files in the Miscellaneous virtual folder to create the destination Schemas:
 - 0_00_BuildConnections.biml
 - 0_20_BuildDestinationSchemasMain.biml

5a. Right-click in Solution Explorer (or dropdown the BimlExpress menu) and click Generate SSIS Packages.

6. In Solution Explorer, multi-select the following Biml files in the Miscellaneous virtual folder to create the destination Tables:
 - 0_00_BuildConnections.biml
 - 0_30_BuildDestinationTablesMain.biml

6a. Right-click in Solution Explorer (or dropdown the BimlExpress menu) and click Generate SSIS Packages.

7. Execute the packages:
 - 10_Build_Destination_Databases.dtsx
 - 20_Build_Destination_Schemas.dtsx
 - 30_Build_Destination_Tables.dtsx

8. Delete all Project Connection Managers and Packages.

9. In Solution Explorer, multi-select the following Biml files in the Miscellaneous virtual folder to create the SSIS Packages:
 - 0_00_BuildConnections.biml
 - 0_10_BuildDestinationDatabaseMain.biml
 - 0_20_BuildDestinationSchemasMain.biml
 - 0_30_BuildDestinationTablesMain.biml
 - 1_99_Main.biml

9a. Right-click in Solution Explorer (or dropdown the BimlExpress menu) and click Generate SSIS Packages.

We have completed Step 0 already.

Restoring the BimlMetadata Database

In SSMS Object Explorer, right-click the Databases node and click Restore Database, as shown in Figure 10-17.

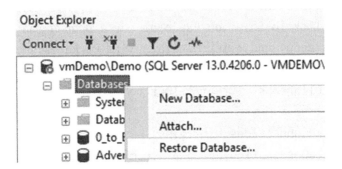

Figure 10-17. *Preparing to restore the BimlMetadata database*

Select the Device option for Source and click the ellipsis to select the backup file. Navigate to the file system folder you extracted the BimlExpressMetadataFramework.zip file from and select the BimlMetadata database backup file, as shown in Figure 10-18.

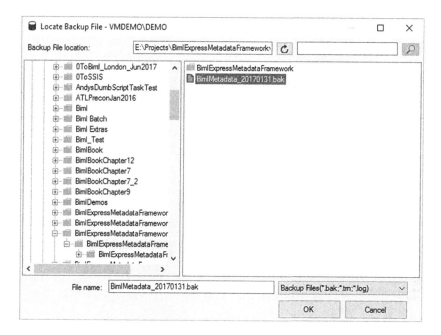

Figure 10-18. *Selecting the BimlMetadata database backup file*

Click the OK button to select the BimlMetadata database backup file and return to the Restore Database dialog, as shown in Figure 10-19.

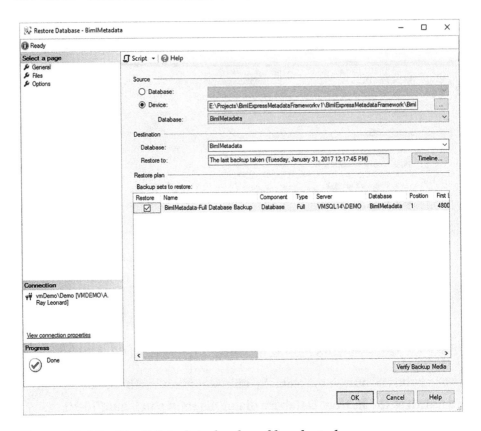

Figure 10-19. *BimlMetadata backup file selected*

Click the Files page and check the "Relocate all files to folder" checkbox. Navigate to the Data and Log file folders, and double-check that the "Restore As" paths match your selections for Data and Log file folders, as shown in Figure 10-20.

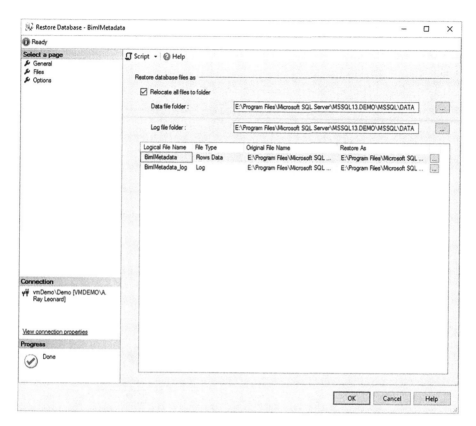

Figure 10-20. *Configuring restore file locations*

On the Options page, check the "Overwrite the existing database (WITH REPLACE)" checkbox, as shown in Figure 10-21.

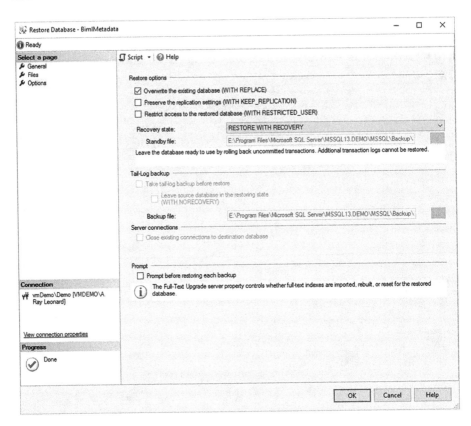

Figure 10-21. *Configuring the restore to overwrite the existing database*

Click the OK button to begin the Database Restore operation.

If all goes as planned, you should see the message box shown in Figure 10-22.

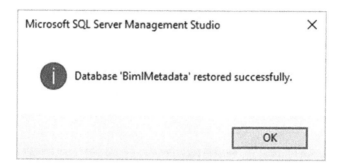

Figure 10-22. *Successful restore!*

Refresh Object Explorer. You should now see the BimlMetadata database listed, as shown in Figure 10-23.

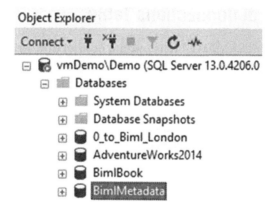

Figure 10-23. *The BimlMetadata database*

If you do not have a copy of the AdventureWorks2014 sample database, search for a download of the Microsoft sample database, download it, and restore or otherwise build it. At the time of this writing, you may obtain a database back file of AdventureWorks2014 at `msftdbprodsamples.codeplex.com/downloads/get/880661`, but Microsoft plans to shut down CodePlex and migrate the code to GitHub.

Updating the Connection String Variable Value in the Params.biml File

The next step in the README file is to update the connection string in the params.biml file to aim it at your BimlMetadata database, as shown in Figure 10-24.

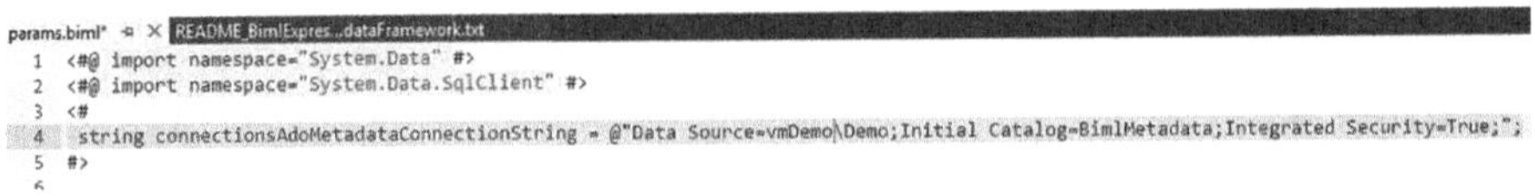

Figure 10-24. *Updating the BimlMetadata connection string in Params.biml*

Updating the di.Connections Table

The next step in the README file is update connection strings in the di. Connections table to aim them at your AdventureWorks2014 database, as shown in Figure 10-25.

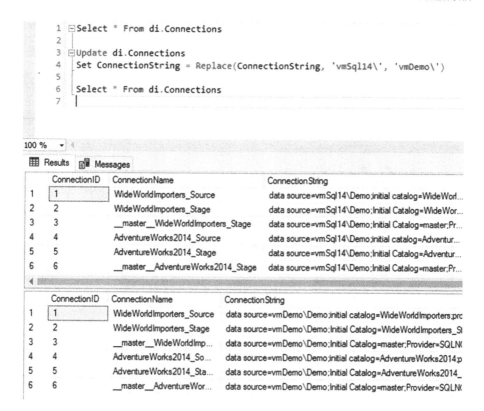

Figure 10-25. *Updating the Adventworks2014 connection strings in the di.Connections table*

Generating the Destination Database

In the BimlExpressMetadataFramework project, multi-select the 0_00_ BuildConnections.biml and 0_10_BuildDestinationDatabaseMain.biml files. Right-click and click Generate SSIS Packages, as shown in Figure 10-26.

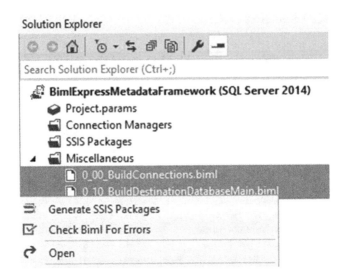

Figure 10-26. *Building the destination database SSIS package*

When the 0_00_BuildConnections.biml and 0_10_
BuildDestinationDatabaseMain.biml files execute, they create the
project connection manager named __master__AdventureWorks2014_
Stage and the SSIS package named 10_Build_Destination_Databases.
dtsx, as shown in Figure 10-27.

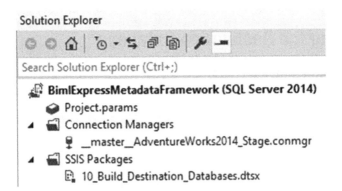

Figure 10-27. *Creating an SSIS package that builds the target*
database

Generating the Destination Schemas

In the BimlExpressMetadataFramework project, multi-select the 0_00_
BuildConnections.biml and 0_20_BuildDestinationSchemasMain.biml
files. Right-click and click Generate SSIS Packages, as shown in Figure 10-28.

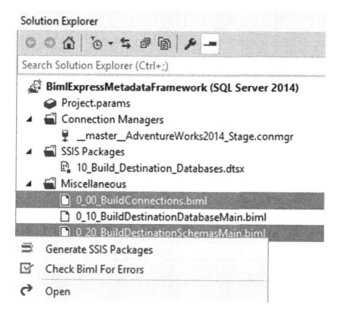

Figure 10-28. *Building the destination schemas SSIS package*

When the 0_00_BuildConnections.biml and 0_20_
BuildDestinationSchemasMain.biml files execute, they create the project
connection manager named AdventureWorks2014_Stage and an SSIS
package named 20_Build_Destination_Schemas.dtsx, as shown in
Figure 10-29.

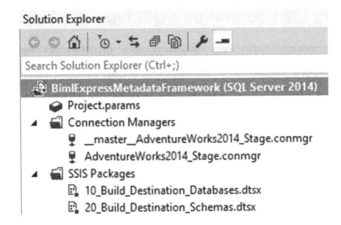

Figure 10-29. *Creating an SSIS package that builds the destination schemas*

Generating the Destination Tables

In the BimlExpressMetadataFramework project, multi-select the 0_00_ BuildConnections.biml and 0_30_BuildDestinationTablesMain.biml files. Right-click and click Generate SSIS Packages, as shown in Figure 10-30.

Figure 10-30. *Building the destination tables SSIS package*

The AdventureWorks2014_Stage project connection manager is regenerated by the 0_30_BuildDestinationTablesMain.biml file. The Confirm Overwritten Items dialog displays as shown in Figure 10-31.

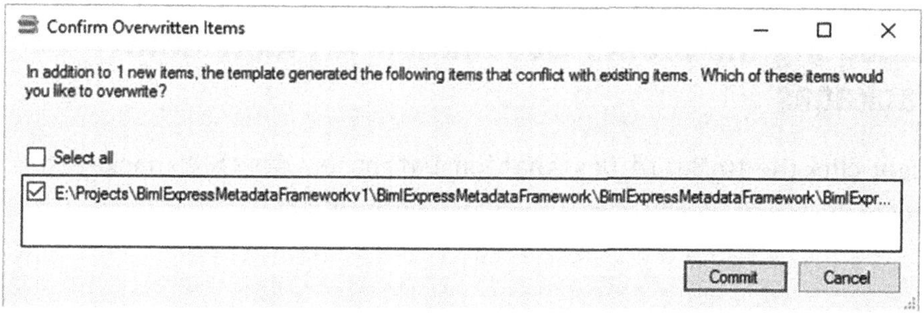

Figure 10-31. *Confirm Overwritten Items dialog*

Click the Commit button to proceed.

When the 0_30_BuildDestinationTablesMain.biml file executes and overwrites the project connection manager, it also overwrites the file named AdventureWorks2014_Stage.conmgr, causing a reload operation, as shown in Figure 10-32.

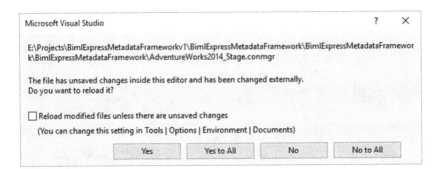

Figure 10-32. *Reloading the overwritten AdventureWorks2014_Stage connection manager file*

Click the Yes button to proceed.

When the 0_00_BuildConnections.biml and 0_30_BuildDestinationTablesMain.biml files execute, they create the project connection manager named AdventureWorks2014_Stage and an SSIS package named 30_Build_Destination_Tables.dtsx.

Executing the Create-Destination-Artifacts SSIS Packages

Right-click the 10_Build_Destination_Databases.dtsx SSIS package to create the target database, as shown in Figure 10-33.

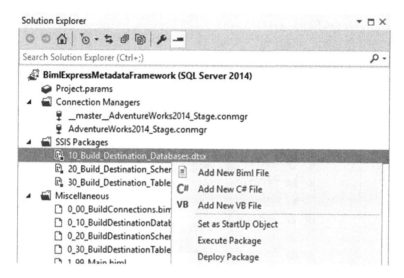

Figure 10-33. *Executing the 10_Build_Destination_Databases.dtsx SSIS package*

If all goes as planned, the 10_Build_Destination_Databases.dtsx SSIS package executes successfully, as shown in Figure 10-34.

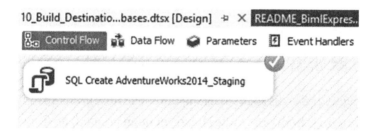

Figure 10-34. *Successful execution of the 10_Build_Destination_ Databases.dtsx SSIS package*

Return to SSMS and refresh the Databases node in Object Explorer, as shown in Figure 10-35.

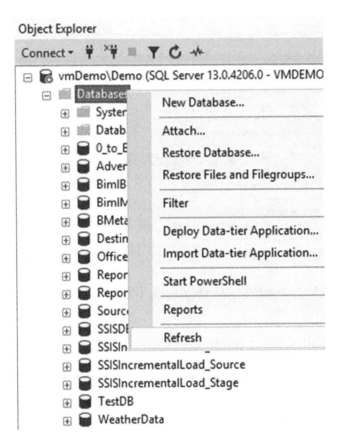

Figure 10-35. *Refreshing the Databases node in Object Explorer*

The AdventureWorks2014_Staging database now appears in the target instance, but no schemas or tables have yet been created, as shown in Figure 10-36.

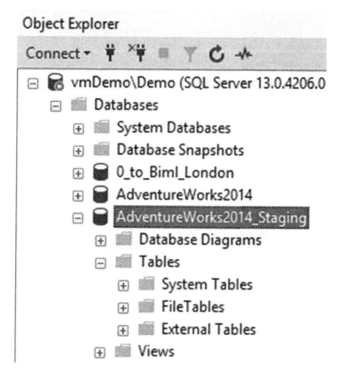

Figure 10-36. *AdventureWorks2014_Staging with no schemas or tables*

Right-click the 20_Build_Destination_Schemas.dtsx SSIS package to create the schemas in the target database, as shown in Figure 10-37.

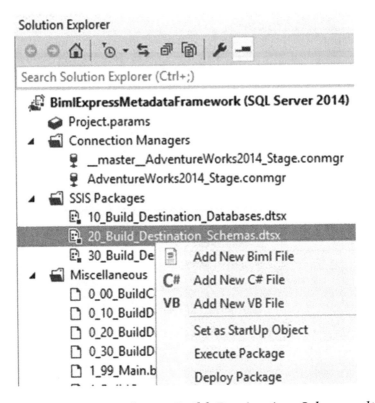

Figure 10-37. *Executing the 20_Build_Destination_Schemas.dtsx SSIS package*

If all goes as planned, the 20_Build_Destination_Schemas.dtsx SSIS package executes successfully, as shown in Figure 10-38.

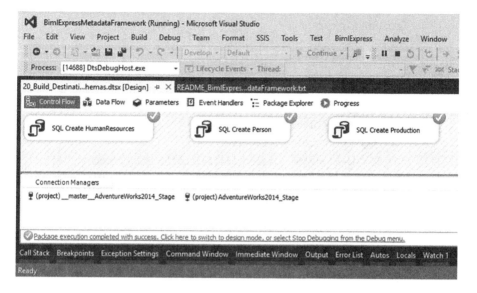

Figure 10-38. *Successful execution of the 20_Build_Destination_
Schemas.dtsx SSIS package*

Right-click the 30_Build_DestinationTables.dtsx SSIS package to
create the tables in the target database, as shown in Figure 10-39.

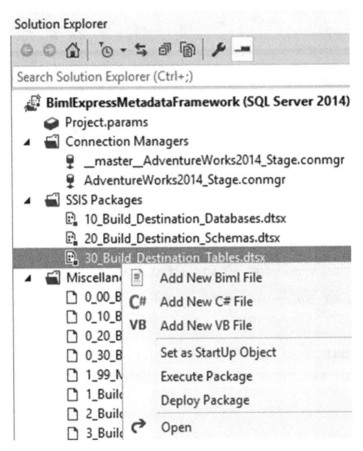

Figure 10-39. *Executing the 30_Build_Destination_Tables.dtsx SSIS package*

If all goes as planned, the 30_Build_Destination_Tables.dtsx SSIS package executes successfully, as shown in Figure 10-40.

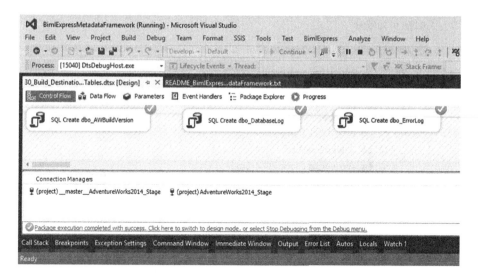

Figure 10-40. *Successful execution of the 30_Build_Destination_
Tables.dtsx SSIS package*

Return to SSMS and refresh the AdventureWorks2014_Staging Tables
node in Object Explorer, as shown in Figure 10-41.

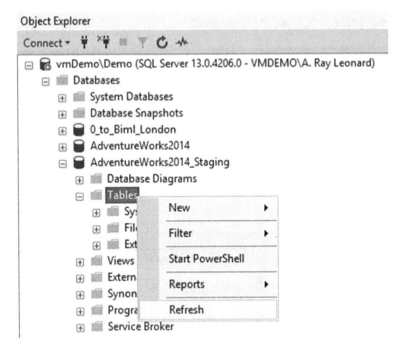

Figure 10-41. *Refreshing the AdventureWorks2014_Staging Tables node*

The AdventureWorks2014_Staging database now contains schemas and tables, as you can see in Figure 10-42.

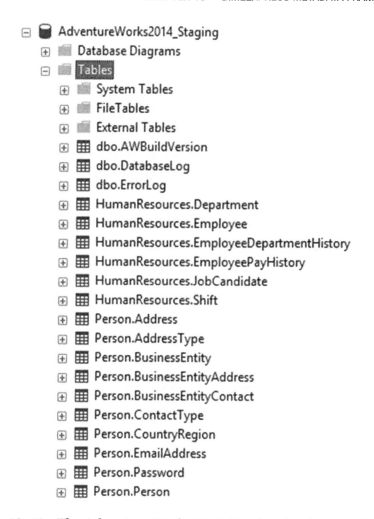

Figure 10-42. *The AdventureWorks2014_Staging database with schemas and tables*

Deleting Existing Artifacts

Delete the existing SSIS packages and project connection managers from the SSIS project, as shown in Figure 10-43.

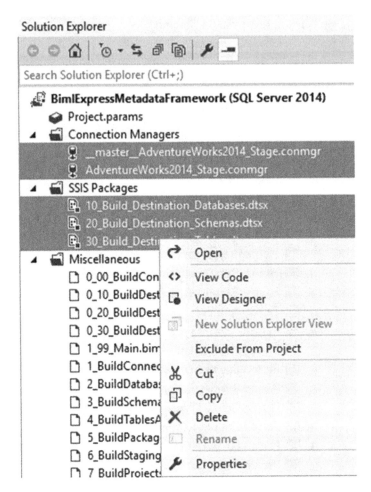

Figure 10-43. *Deleting the existing artifacts*

You do not have to delete the existing artifacts. If you do not delete the existing artifacts, BimlExpress will prompt you to confirm overwrites of existing artifacts.

Generating SSIS Packages

Multi-select 0_00_BuildConnections.biml,
0_10_BuildDestinationDatabaseMain.biml,
0_20_BuildDestinationSchemasMain.biml, 0_30_

BuildDestinationTablesMain.biml, and 1_99_Main.biml. Right-click and select Generate SSIS Packages, as shown in Figure 10-44.

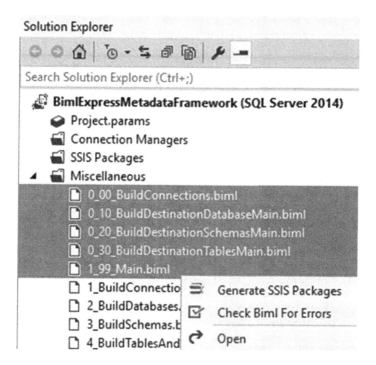

Figure 10-44. *Generating SSIS packages*

As before, when generating the Destination Tables SSIS package, you will be prompted to overwrite the AdventureWorks2014_Stage project connection manager and its file. The process generates 75 SSIS packages in all:

  1 Create Destination database

  1 Create Destination schemas

  1 Create Destination tables

  71 SSIS loaders, one for each table in the AdventureWorks2014 database

  1 controller that contains 71 Execute Package tasks, one for each SSIS loader

Please see Figure 10-45.

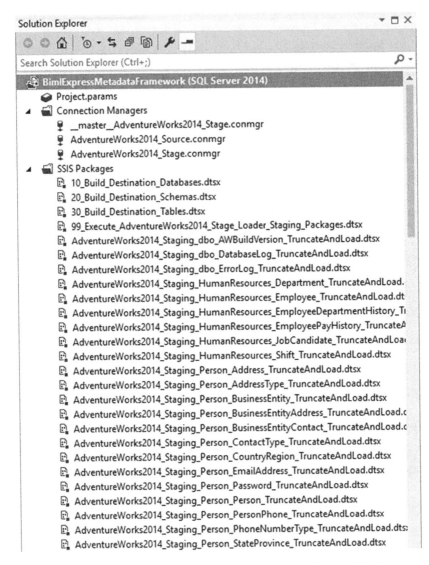

Figure 10-45. *AdventureWorks2014 Staging SSIS complete!*

Executing the Controller

Execute the Controller SSIS package named 99_Execute_AdventureWorks 2014_Stage_Loader_Staging_Packages.dtsx, as shown in Figure 10-46.

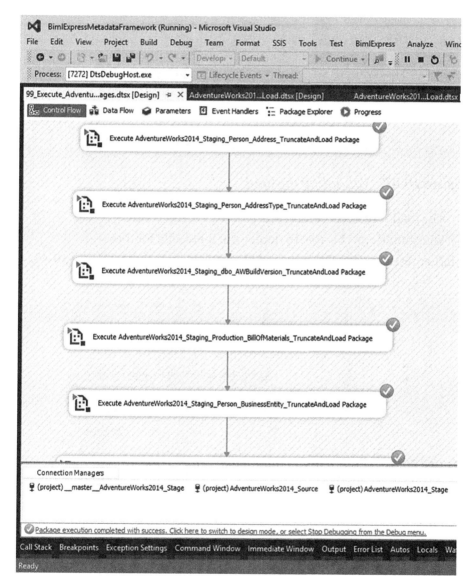

Figure 10-46. *Executing the Controller SSIS package*

Validating the Load

In SSMS, run a few test queries to validate the load process executed successfully, as shown in Figure 10-47.

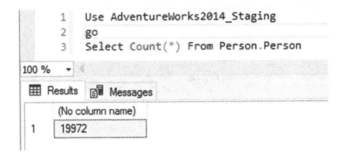

Figure 10-47. *Validating the load*

The load process is validated.

You should now be able to deploy the ISPAC file for the BimlExpressMetadataFramework SSIS project, as shown in Figure 10-48.

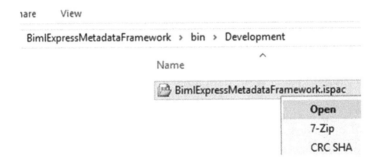

Figure 10-48. *Preparing to deploy the BimlExpressMetadata Framework ISPAC file*

Full Circle

You've come full circle in this demo. You deployed an SSIS project to an SSIS catalog in Chapter 3. In Chapter 7, you executed a script that added metadata to SSIS Framework Community Edition for an SSIS catalog project, an SSIS project already deployed to an SSIS catalog, which allowed you to execute all of the SSIS packages that were part of the SSIS catalog project by calling a single stored procedure and passing it a single parameter value.

CHAPTER 11

Conclusion

As shipped, SQL Server Integration Services (SSIS) is ready for enterprise data integration, but not as ready for enterprise DevOps and data integration lifecycle management (DILM). Using the best practices, tools, and utilities outlined in this book, you can deliver data integration solutions that participate in enterprise DevOps.

The collection of free, free and open-source, and for-sale utilities available at DILM Suite are built to support enterprise data integration lifecycle management for enterprises using SSIS for data integration.

© Andy Leonard 2018
A. Leonard, *Data Integration Life Cycle Management with SSIS*,
https://doi.org/10.1007/978-1-4842-3276-7_11

APPENDIX A

Links

SQL Server Developer Edition

microsoft.com/en-us/sql-server/application-development

SQL Server Management Studio (SSMS)

docs.microsoft.com/en-us/sql/ssms/download-sql-
server-management-studio-ssms

SQL Server Data Tools (SSDT)

docs.microsoft.com/en-us/sql/ssdt/download-sql-server-data-
tools-ssdt

SQL Server Central Stairway to Integration Services

sqlservercentral.com/stairway/72494/

Visual Studio Online

visualstudio.com

Team Foundation Services (TFS)

visualstudio.com/en-us/docs/tools

"Deploying SSIS Projects to a Restored SSIS Catalog (SSISDB)"

andyleonard.blog/2017/07/29/deploying-ssis-projects-to-
a-restored-ssis-catalog-ssisdb

© Andy Leonard 2018
A. Leonard, *Data Integration Life Cycle Management with SSIS*,
https://doi.org/10.1007/978-1-4842-3276-7_12

Catalog Browser

dilmsuite.com/catalog-browser

SSIS Catalog Compare

dilmsuite.com/ssis-catalog-compare

SSIS Framework Community Edition

dilmsuite.com/ssis-framework-community-edition

"Adding an SSIS Application to SSIS Framework Community Edition"

andyleonard.blog/2017/07/26/adding-an-ssis-application-
to-ssis-framework-community-edition

Framework Browser

dilmsuite.com/framework-browser

Catalog Reports

dilmsuite.com/catalog-reports

Biml

varigence.com/biml and bimlscript.com

BimlExpress

varigence.com/bimlexpress

BimlExpress Metadata Framework

dilmsuite.com/biml-express-metadata-framework

AdventureWorks2014

msftdbprodsamples.codeplex.com/downloads/get/880661

Erratum to: Introduction to DILM

Andy Leonard

Erratum to:

Chapter 1 in: Andy Leonard, *Data Integration Life Cycle Management with SSIS,* https://doi.org/10.1007/978-1-4842-3276-7_1

The original version of this book was published with incorrect Chapter title in Chapter 1. It has been corrected and updated as: Introduction to DILM.

The updated original online version for this book can be found at
https://doi.org/10.1007/978-1-4842-3276-7_1

© Andy Leonard 2018
A. Leonard, *Data Integration Life Cycle Management with SSIS,*
https://doi.org/10.1007/978-1-4842-3276-7_13

Index

A

Application lifecycle management (ALM), 1
Application packages, 129

B

BimlExpress Metadata Framework
    downloading
        BimlExpressMetadata
        Framework.sln file,
        open, 146
        extract file, 144–145
        file extension, 143
        rename file, 143
        text file, 142
    installation
        extensions and
        updates, 141
        license agreement,
        accept, 140
    README file instructions
        controller execution, 173
        deleting existing artifacts,
        169–170
        destination database, 155–156
        destination schemas, 157–158
        destination tables, 158–160

di.Connections table,
    updating, 154–155
executing, destination-
    artifacts SSIS packages (see
    README file instructions,
    destination-artifacts SSIS
    packages)
load validation, 174
notes, 146
restoring, BimlMetadata
    Database, 153
SSIS packages generating,
    170–172
updating BimlMetadata
    connection string, Params.
    biml, 154
viewing, SSDT, 138
Branching, 26
Business Intelligence Markup
    Language (Biml), 5, 137

C

Catalog browser
    catalog properties, 94
    description, 87
    environment variables, data
        types, and values, 92

© Andy Leonard 2018
A. Leonard, *Data Integration Life Cycle Management with SSIS*,
https://doi.org/10.1007/978-1-4842-3276-7

T, U

V, W, X, Y, Z

Get the eBook for only $5!

Why limit yourself?

With most of our titles available in both PDF and ePUB format, you can access your content wherever and however you wish—on your PC, phone, tablet, or reader.

Since you've purchased this print book, we are happy to offer you the eBook for just $5.

To learn more, go to http://www.apress.com/companion or contact support@apress.com.

Apress®

Printed in the United States
By Bookmasters